FROM DUBLIN TO NEW ORLEANS

Nora and Alice's Journey to America 1889

[handwritten inscription:] For Jane— With warm regards, Suellen Oct. 1999

Suellen Hoy
and
Margaret MacCurtain

Attic Press
DUBLIN

© Suellen Hoy and Margaret MacCurtain 1994

All rights reserved. Except for brief passages quoted in newspaper, magazine, radio or television reviews, no part of this book may be reproduced in any form or by any means, electronic or mechanical, including photocopying or recording, or by any information storage and retrieval systems without prior permission from the Publishers.

First published in Ireland in 1994 by
Attic Press
4 Upper Mount Street
Dublin 2

British Library Cataloguing in Publication Data
Hoy, Suellen and MacCurtain, Margaret
From Dublin to New Orleans: Journey of Nora and Alice
I. Title II. Hoy Suellen
305.4092

ISBN 1-85594-089-2

The moral right of Suellen Hoy and Margaret MacCurtain to be identified as the authors of this work is asserted.

Cover Design: Syd Bluett
Origination: Verbatim Typesetting and Design
Printing: Guernsey Press Co Ltd

This book is published with the assistance of The Arts Council/An Chomhairle Ealaíon

DEDICATION

To all the Irish women who emigrated
for religious purposes

ABOUT THE AUTHORS

Suellen Hoy is a scholar and historian who lives in Indiana. She is currently completing a book on the history of cleanliness in the USA.

Margaret MacCurtain, a Dominican Sister, lectures in the History Department in UCD and was one of the founders of Women's Studies in that university. She is one of Ireland's leading historians.

ACKNOWLEDGEMENTS

This book is at heart Irish-American. Nora and Alice, to be sure, were Irish but they lived nearly half their lives in America. Suellen Hoy, one author, is American; while the other, Margaret MacCurtain, is Irish. And, most importantly, the archivists whose assistance was essential to this collaborative project are Irish and American: Sister Terence O'Keeffe at the Dominican Sisters Archives at Cabra and Sister Dorothy Dawes at the Dominican Sisters Archives (Congregation of St Mary) at New Orleans.

Institutions on both sides of the Atlantic have also been supportive. During 1991–2 Hoy received two research fellowships to study the recruitment and emigration of Irish religious women to the United States, 1812–1914 (her findings will be published as 'The Journey Out' in the *Journal of Women's History*, Indiana University Press, Bloomington, Indiana, USA). In the course of that research, she came across Nora and Alice's diaries; thus they are, in a sense, a part of the larger project funded by the Irish American Cultural Institute, St Paul, Minnesota, and the Cushwa Center for the Study of American Catholicism at the University of Notre Dame; to both of them, grateful thanks for much needed support. University College Dublin, where MacCurtain is a faculty member, also gave Hoy faculty research privileges during 1991–2, for which she remains appreciative. And, finally, the John J. Burns Library, Boston College, where MacCurtain held the Burns Chair of Irish Studies in 1992–3, made it possible for the authors to complete their work in an expeditious manner.

Along the way toward completion, numerous individuals have been especially interested and helpful to us. The Nolans and Prendivilles in Castleisland, County Kerry, could not have been more cordial to the two strangers who knocked on their doors in the spring of 1992. Hannah Prendiville, who is now deceased but who had been married to Nora's youngest brother, provided us with critical information at an early stage of our research. We are also grateful to the Presentation Sisters (especially Sisters Virgilius Flavin and Margaret O'Brien) at Saints Stephen and John Parish in Castleisland who made available national school records from the 1870s and 1880s. And we thank two Dominicans—Sister Darina Hosey, Regional Vicar, and Sister Marian O'Sullivan, Prioress General—for granting us permission to publish Nora and Alice's diaries.

We also express our appreciation to Norman J. G. Pounds, cartographer and historian-geographer at Cambridge University, who graciously prepared and donated the maps; to Andrew Simons, reference archivist at the Amistad Research Center in New Orleans, for assisting us with photographs; to Róisín Conroy and Gráinne Healy at Attic Press, who immediately liked our project and recognized its significance; and last, but hardly least, Walter Nugent, historian at the University of Notre Dame and author of *Crossings: The Great Transatlantic Migrations, 1870–1914*, who served as a knowledgeable and amiable special consultant.

CONTENTS

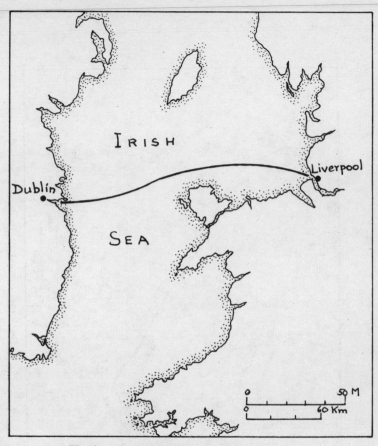

The first stage of the voyage of Nora and Alice

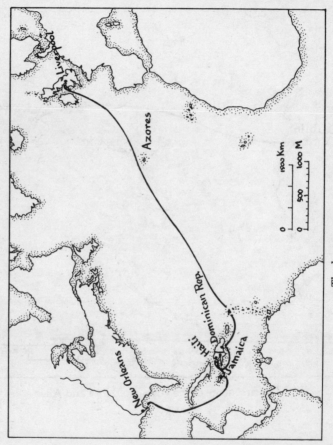

The long ocean voyage

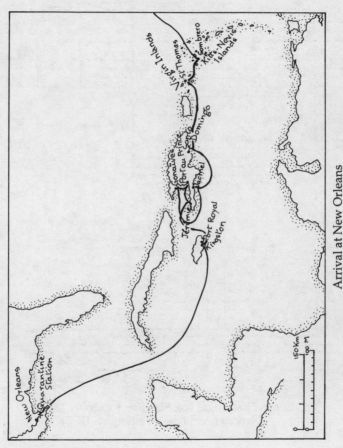

Arrival at New Orleans

Passenger List

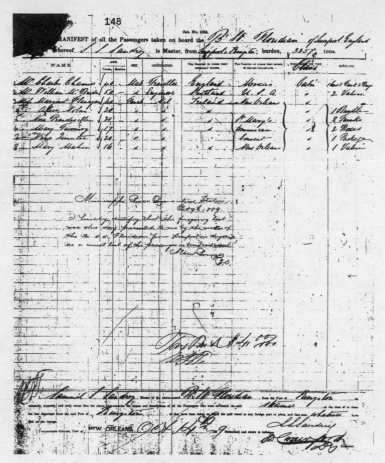

Copy of passenger list, *Floridian*, 9 October 1889
(National Archives, Washington DC)

PREFACE

Nora and Alice's diaries do, in fact, exist. They are located in Dublin at the Dominican Sisters' Archives at Cabra. The two simple, black, schoolgirl notebooks—unnamed and undated, except for the daily entries—are in the good care of Sister Terence O'Keeffe, who made them available to me for the first time on 2 December 1991. From that day on, they became lodged in my thoughts and a part of my discussions with friends and acquaintances until, about three months later, an *Irish Times* review of a published diary written by a wealthy eighteenth-century woman prompted me to act. I telephoned Margaret MacCurtain, a member of the Department of Modern Irish History at University College Dublin and a Dominican herself, and told her about the diaries. She subsequently read them and, like me, found them fascinating—more interesting than the eighteenth-century record by an Irish lady of the landed gentry.

We were, however, puzzled. Who were Nora and Alice—other than two 'Cabra girls' who journeyed out to New Orleans to become Dominican Sisters? When did they make their voyage, why did they write 'diaries,' and why were these diaries at Cabra and not in New Orleans? Other questions followed quickly but, almost immediately, we began to wonder what happened to Nora and Alice. Did they

13

actually become nuns, did they remain their entire lives in New Orleans, and did they ever see Ireland again? Our curiosity was piqued; our quest had begun.

In an attempt to answer a whole array of questions, we made several more research trips to the archives at Cabra in early 1992, and we travelled twice to the south-west of Ireland after discovering that Nora and Alice had been born there. In 1993 we also visited the Dominican Sisters in New Orleans, where Sister Dorothy Dawes ably assisted us in our pursuit of information on Nora and Alice. What you will read in the following pages will acquaint you with a largely untold emigration story—one paralleled by thousands of young, single women who left Ireland to serve God and the millions of Irish people who had gone before them in search of a better life for themselves and their families. Nora and Alice were just two among many ordinary, talented and adventuresome Irish women who, in emigrating to help others, found useful and satisfying lives for themselves.

Nora and Alice's diaries, which are the main part of this book, have been left largely as we found them. They were, of course, handwritten and in black ink; they had few misspellings. Where such errors did exist, we have corrected them in the belief that in doing so we have not altered Nora and Alice's thoughts. We have omitted any word or group of words that were crossed out in the original, and we have tried to make punctuation and capitalisation less idiosyncratic. Nora and Alice often used commas instead of periods and frequently did not capitalise words at the beginning of sentences. There are some

14

minor discrepancies between the two accounts, but we have not corrected them. Contradictions, inconsistencies, and repetitions, we have concluded, give readers a much better feel for the diaries as Nora and Alice wrote them.

Suellen Hoy

PART I

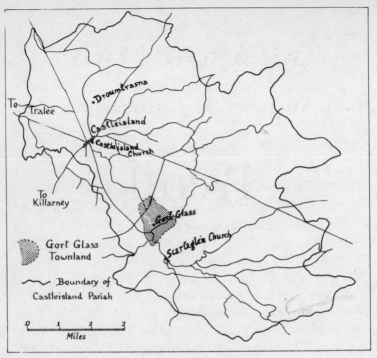

Castleisland, County Kerry
Nora's Home: Gort Glass
Alice's home: Droumtrasna

Two Among Many:

Nora, Alice and the American Vocation

Suellen Hoy

In September and early October of 1889, Honoria Prendiville (1868–1907) and Alicia Joseph Nolan (1869–1910) made their way across the Atlantic on board the steamship *Floridian*. They began their journey on a ferry at Dublin's North Wall, crossed the Irish Sea, and, despite a series of upsets, found themselves in the good hands of Captain Samuel S. Sandrey, an Englishman who would become their friend and teacher, on a month-long journey from Liverpool to New Orleans. Nora and Alice's diaries record their adventures on an ocean path that took them on an unusual voyage through the West Indies. They begin with their poignant departure from the Dominican boarding school, Immaculata, at Cabra in north Dublin, that had become 'school-home' to these two young women from Castleisland, County Kerry.[1]

Nora and Alice, although quite different personalities, led very similar lives and forged what seems a unique bond of friendship. Both girls were born in Castleisland in the late 1860s to fairly prosperous farm families who owned their own land—land that even today is farmed by the

Prendivilles at Gort Glass and the Nolans at Droumtrasna (see map of Castleisland parish). They were both baptised at Saints Stephen and John Catholic Church and attended the national school, next door to the church, run by the Presentation Sisters. Nora and Alice left Castleisland for Dublin as young women to become boarders at Cabra. Although a year younger than Nora, Alice arrived at Cabra first in 1885 at the age of sixteen; Nora followed two years later, when she was nineteen. There they lived, except for short summer vacations, until they went to New Orleans in 1889. As Dominican Sisters in New Orleans, they taught school near their convent on Dryades Street, where they both died at an early age. Nora, who became Sister Patricia, died of tuberculosis in 1907 at thirty-nine; Alice, then known as Sister Columba (or, more affectionately, 'Dovey'), died of carditis three years later. Both are buried in New Orleans.[2]

Despite the fact that they died young, Nora and Alice demonstrated at the ages of twenty-one and twenty a desire to make the *most* and the *best* of life. High-spirited and curious, they displayed their adaptability, inquisitiveness, and pluckiness while crossing the Atlantic on a coaling vessel. Within a week of their departure, they had not only recovered from their seasickness but had also become 'quite at home on the sea.' They had made friends with the captain and some of the crew through their never-ending questions about nautical instruments and ship life, and they openly admitted that they were 'enjoying [their] time immensely.'

While neither Nora nor Alice appeared unusually devout or religious, they both manifested loyalty to

Ireland and the cause of Home Rule as well as to Cabra and its 'inmates.' Alice, although a year younger than Nora, had been at Immaculata longer and was far more a 'Cabra girl.' It is obvious from Alice's diary that she had been very happy at boarding school and felt especially close to 'dear Mother Prioress and the dear good sisters' there. (In New Orleans she would be given the name of one of her teachers, Sister Mary Columba.) Alice was, in fact, a dutiful, serious, and 'faithful child of St Mary's.' What her diary does not reveal is that she had two blood-sisters, Ellie and Bridget, who remained students at Cabra. These facts explain why Alice so longingly recalled 'old times' and insisted on keeping 'Cabra time' until she arrived in New Orleans.[3]

Nora was neither as sentimental nor as nostalgic. She seems, however, more buoyant, self-assured, and direct. She was the second eldest girl in a family of eleven children and, during her years in the Presentation Sisters' school, received excellent grades. Nora left Castleisland at nineteen, not sixteen, to attend Immaculata; and, although it is not clear why she selected the Dominicans at Cabra, she probably enrolled with some intention of becoming a nun. Alice, whose uncle and godfather was the parish priest at Lixnaw from 1876 to 1893, knew the Dominicans well; she had an older half-sister, Mary Julia, who was a Dominican at the Siena Convent in Drogheda.[4]

The Dominican presence in County Kerry was centuries old. The Dominican Priory at Tralee was founded in 1272 and, during penal times, the Dominicans preached and said Mass in hideouts in the Castleisland-Scartaglin area of Kerry. Castle-island, where both Nora and Alice were born and spent their childhoods, was (and is) a small market town—with an unusually wide main street—located in the rolling farmlands between Killarney and Tralee. During the early 1880s, Castleisland became known in Ireland and England for its active Land League branch and a series of 'agrarian disturbances' (Nora refers to them as 'the agitation') on behalf of Charles Stewart Parnell and his efforts to secure Home Rule for Ireland. Although Parnell did not visit Castleisland, he sent Michael Davitt to stop the violence, 'the abominable outrages,' in 1886. By that time, a railway linked Castleisland to Tralee, where local trains connected with the Great Southern and Western. Thus, travel to and from Dublin, where the Dominican Sisters had opened a school at Cabra for 'young ladies' in 1835, became a reasonable and manageable choice for daughters of the rural bourgeoisie that emerged after the Famine.[5]

When Nora and Alice arrived at Cabra in the 1880s, Immaculata accommodated seventy pupils ranging in age from seven to nineteen. The school was entering a long period of distinction and was, even then, drawing girls and young women from every part of the country. Successor to the Channel Row 'venture' of taking children within the enclosure of the convent as boarders—something the Dominican nuns had done in 1719 in defiance of the penal legislation—the Cabra boarding school was the third and final expression of an idea that the Dominicans had managed to keep alive for well over a century. It was, for them, a proud achievement since they had accomplished it despite severe shortages of money and teachers.[6]

Immaculata consisted of two wings built in successive stages on either side of St Mary's Convent, a Georgian residence the nuns had acquired in 1819. The boarding school continued the Georgian architecture of the convent and, when completed, created a semi-circular Palladian effect. Inside the entrance—an arched gateway frequently sketched by art students—boarders and visitors found 'a lawn beautified by some of the most magnificent trees'; and beyond the landscaped gardens, they saw fields that stretched a long distance towards a railway and canal. Seven miles from the centre of Dublin, Cabra was rich farmland that must have made Nora and Alice feel at ease.[7]

From the school's beginning, the Dominican nuns promised parents that their daughters would leave Immaculata 'fit for usefulness in their future stations.'[8] For an annual fee of £30, according to an advertisement for the school in the *Irish Catholic Directory*, pupils learned—besides religion—'the usual branches of English Education, Viz.,— Grammar, History, Geography, Astronomy, the use of the Globes, Writing and Arithmetic; French and Italian Languages; and every species of Plain and Ornamental Needle Work.' The prospectus offered several extra benefits to those who wished to pay: music at two guineas a quarter, singing and dancing lessons at £2 each a season, and classes in drawing at £1.10 a quarter. In addition each 'young lady' was asked to bring two pair of sheets, two pillow cases, four towels, four napkins, a knife, silver fork, and teaspoon (all to be returned when the students left

Cabra). The school provided uniforms but charged £2 a year for laundry. Vacation time lasted only a month, from 23 July to 23 August.[9]

Educated well by the Presentation Sisters in Castleisland and hard-working students at Cabra, Nora and Alice maintained an enviable level of performance. They appeared on Immaculata's 1889 Honours List for religion, arithmetic, French, English, drawing, and needlework—though not for music, natural philosophy, or Italian; and both received a 'first prize' for diligence. Cabra boarders also participated in a variety of activities that occupied the after-school hours. In 1888 Alice was cited for her part in the school play, *The Children of the Castle*. The previous year Immaculata had performed Mendelssohn's Oratorio, *Elijah*, in which every student seems to have taken part.[10]

Boarding school life in a Catholic convent setting mirrored the nuns' routine in many ways. The rising bell rang at 6.45 in the morning to the sound of a nun's voice intoning 'Praise to the Lord Jesus Christ' to which the sleepy dormitory responded 'Amen.' All, except the sick, attended Mass at 7.20, followed by breakfast eaten in silence, morning prayers, and exercise out of doors before the beginning of classes at 9.30. After a short lunch break, during which students could talk to their friends, classes resumed at 12.30 and finished at 2.30. Dinner was promptly served, and boarders then had an hour of recreation. At 4.00 pupils reported to the study hall and remained there until 6.00, when they recited the Rosary. Tea (or supper) followed, as did another hour of study. At 8.30 a convivial half hour ended the day before the 9.00 bell rang for night prayers and bedtime. Elocution, singing, and play rehearsal took place during study time. Saturdays brought two hours of mending and sewing. The boarders took long walks on Sundays and were allowed to read books, both non-fiction and fiction, from the library.[11]

Adjacent to Immaculata were two schools—one for deaf children and a 'free' school for neighbourhood young people of poor circumstances. The Vincentian Fathers served as school chaplains and usually conducted the annual three-day retreat. That was the spiritual peak of the school year, designed to finish on Rosary Sunday, the one closest to the Feast of the Holy Rosary on the seventh of October. The school year was also punctuated by a series of special religious services—monthly novenas and the new devotion of *Quarantore* or Forty Hours introduced into Immaculata in 1887.[12]

When the strangeness of life at Immaculata wore off and the unfamiliar became routine, Nora and Alice found kindness and inspiration in their teachers. In their diaries, both young women show a fondness for Sister Catherine de Ricci Maher, who served as the Mother Prioress from 1887 to 1893. She came from Carlow, was a member of the same family as Ireland's first cardinal (Paul Cullen), and lived until 1899. Not long before her death, a former Cabra pupil wrote a letter that provides some insight into the relationships that formed between Sister Catherine de Ricci (and probably the other nuns too) and the boarders:

Mother de Ricci spent a long time with us...and just as of old was anxious to know how we should like to spend the play day, where we

should like to go, and what we should like to
do...to secure our happiness and enjoyment
seemed her greatest pleasure.[13]

Nora and Alice adapted so well to life at
Immaculata that some time in 1889 they decided to
become Dominican Sisters. What is perhaps more
surprising is their second decision—they chose to
journey out to America, leaving behind their real
homes in Kerry and their adopted home at Cabra.
But, when they left their 'school-home' for New
Orleans, they carried with them recollections of
solicitous teachers and friendly companions. In
memory, as their diaries indicate, they often strolled
along on Cabra's 'New Lime Walk.' And for the rest
of their lives they probably compared every church
they visited (as they did in St Thomas, Virgin Islands)
with the elegant marble chapel at Immaculata or with
the equally fine church in Castleisland, opened and
consecrated when they were schoolchildren there.

Nora and Alice were hardly the first Irishwomen
to journey out to America for religious purposes.
Since the beginning of the nineteenth century,
countless numbers of young women had gone out to
the New World. The first wave began in 1812 when a
group of Ursuline nuns travelled from Cork to New
York, where they established the initial foundation of
Irish religious women in America. Numerous
religious communities followed their example and
sent out—usually at the invitation of Irish-born
bishops and priests in America—small groups of
professed Sisters to bring the faith and minister to the
needs of the millions of Irish who emigrated before,
during, and after the Famine.

Although the first wave of religious emigrants would continue into the 1880s, a second wave began during the late 1860s and lasted well into the twentieth century. Young Irishwomen, the majority of whom were not professed nuns or even novices, responded to the appeals of religious women (often Irish nuns who had previously emigrated) sent to Ireland in the spring and summer months to recruit new members. In this way, several thousand women travelled to America, usually as aspirants, to enter religious orders and receive training for their lifelong work. Nora and Alice were just two among many.[14]

During the summer of 1889, the Dominicans at Cabra welcomed an old friend, Margaret (or 'Maddie' as everyone called her) Flanagan. Maddie was the blood-sister of Mother Mary John Flanagan, the founder and superior of the Dominican foundation in New Orleans. Mother Mary John had been a member of the Cabra community until 1860, when Father Jeremiah Moynihan, pastor of St John the Baptist Church in New Orleans, invited the Dominicans to open a school in his parish. Father Moynihan was a friend of Father Patrick Flanagan, pastor of St Patrick's Church in New Orleans and cousin to Mother Mary John. Perhaps it was for this reason that she was selected, at the age of thirty-three, to lead a group of six to America.[15]

Twenty-nine years later, when Mother Mary John sent her sister Maddie to Dublin, the Dominican Sisters in New Orleans had three schools. A month after their arrival, in December 1860, they had opened St John the Baptist School for Girls (Christian Brothers taught the boys) on Dryades Street. During the following year, despite the outbreak of Civil War, the Sisters founded St Mary's Dominican Academy in the Dryades Street convent, and in 1863 it became a boarding school. Two years later the nuns purchased property in the suburb of Greenville, moved the boarders there from their crowded quarters on Dryades Street in 1865, and turned St Mary's Academy into a day school for young women.[16]

Although the Sisters' responsibilities had grown from one school to three, they ran them under extreme financial difficulties, especially during the 1870s and 1880s. Their problems began when they agreed to mortgage their convent so that Father Moynihan could replace a provisional wooden church with a much larger one of brick. In 1874, when Father Moynihan resigned as pastor, his successor and the Dominican nuns inherited some very large debts. In the depressed economy of the war-ravaged South, it became nearly impossible to buy back their own convent. In an attempt to do so, the nuns not only ate sparingly but resorted to 'collecting tours' through city streets. Not until 1894 did they successfully achieve their goal.[17]

Overworked and understaffed, Mother Mary John needed 'useful subjects,' especially ones who were energetic and educated. In addition to her usual pleas for recruits, she sent her sixty-year-old sister, Maddie, to Cabra in the summer of 1889. Margaret Flanagan was not a Dominican nun. She had come to New Orleans in 1877 with another sister, Jane, who subsequently became Sister Mary Catherine. But Maddie, who some thought resembled Queen Victoria in appearance, chose to remain outside the cloister ('enclosure' among Dominicans and other Old World religious orders gradually disappeared as the ministries of 'American' nuns became larger and more active). As a lay tertiary, she conducted the business transactions of everyday life; she carried mail between the Dryades Street convent and the one in Greenville, for instance, and purchased food and provisions for both places. In September 1889 'Miss Flanagan,' as she is referred to in Nora and Alice's diaries, escorted five Irish aspirants to New Orleans.[18]

Besides Nora and Alice, who shared a cabin on board the *Floridian*, and Miss Flanagan, three other women made the trip. Nora Quilter, twenty years old and a native of Scartaglin in County Kerry, was something of an 'outsider.' It is uncertain how she became a part of Nora and Alice's group since she did not emigrate to become a Dominican. Instead she became a Marianite Sister of the Holy Cross, later served as provincial superior of its Louisiana Province, and lived until 1954. Since Scartaglin is a neighbouring townland to Castleisland and since Nora Quilter went to the Presentation Sisters' national school for one year, it is likely that the Quilters would have known the Prendivilles or the Nolans. But Nora Quilter was not a 'Cabra girl.'[19]

Mary Twomey and Mary Mahon, seventeen and sixteen years of age, were a good deal younger than Nora and Alice and seem not to have known them. Mary Twomey (later Sister Mary Benignus) appears to have come from Cabra, but her name is not listed in the boarding school account book. She did, however, have a cousin at Cabra who was a professed Sister. Like Nora and Alice, Mary Twomey was born in Castleisland and attended the Presentation Sisters' school there. Her connection with Cabra, however, remains a mystery. Sister Benignus unfortunately died of tuberculosis in 1891 at the age of nineteen, two years after arriving in New Orleans. Mary Mahon was born in Dublin and had an aunt who was a lay Sister (Sister Martha) at Cabra. Following her example, Mary became Sister Martha in New Orleans and lived as 'a humble lay Sister' until 1905. She worked as the gatekeeper at the entrance to St Mary's Dominican Academy in Greenville and served hot lunches to the boarders in their dining room.[20]

Lay Sisters were responsible for 'life-maintaining' tasks. They cooked and cleaned, washed and ironed, answered the door, served hot meals, and did whatever else needed to be done to keep a well-ordered home and boarding school. It was their work that made it possible for the Noras and Alices to teach, nurse, or carry out other activities encouraged by the Rules of the religious order to which they all belonged.

But work was not the only way in which the lives of lay and choir Sisters differed. The former were not required to recite the Divine Office, even when it was said in English; and lay Sisters frequently took simple vows in religious communities that had solemn ones. They usually dressed differently from choir Sisters (lay Dominicans wore all black habits or black scapulars instead of white ones) and sometimes ate before or after them, not with them. In rank, lay Sisters followed the most junior choir Sister; and in convent elections, lay Sisters could not vote or hold office.

Lay Sisters dated from the Middle Ages, when it was customary for wealthy women who entered the cloister to bring maids with them. However, only the wealthy contributed large dowries; and, because these women came from ruling families who were educated, only they were capable of reading the Latin prayers of the Divine Office. In nineteenth-century Irish convents, lay Sisters, for the most part, came from working-class families who could provide only a small dowry or none at all. Also, lay Sisters were usually less well educated than choir Sisters. In fact, by the 1880s, 'education' generally replaced 'dowry' as the critical word when Irishwomen were recruited for American convents.[21]

Nora and Alice were educated women from middle-class families. Unfortunately, there is no record to indicate what financial arrangement took place between them, their families, and the Dominican Sisters. It is possible, particularly since Nora and Alice had separate first-class cabins and relatively free rein on the *Floridian*, that they had paid their own way. But, because of the particular circumstances of the Prendivilles and Nolans in 1889, it is unlikely that Nora and Alice brought dowries to the New Orleans Dominicans equal to the £200 that Mother Mary John Flanagan brought to Cabra when she entered the Dominicans in 1845.[22] The question of dowry, more than likely, explains why Nora and Alice chose to leave Cabra. It still required a cash dowry; New Orleans did not.

John and Julia Prendiville were substantial farmers, but they were also the parents of seven daughters and four sons. The eldest daughter, Julia, died at an early age. Nora was the second eldest, and over time she assisted her family by bringing out two of her younger sisters, Nell and Maggie, to New

Orleans. They too became Dominicans. Bessie and Kate also became nuns; the former joined the Presentation Sisters in Australia and the latter joined the Sisters of Saint Joseph of Peace in England. Minnie, who lived until she was seventy-four, did not become a nun nor did she marry. Unless the Prendivilles had sold most of what they owned, they probably would not have been able to provide dowries for all of their daughters.[23]

The Nolans' circumstances were more complicated. Martin Nolan, Alice's father, died in January 1889—nine months before she left for New Orleans. Alice's mother, Ellen Sullivan Nolan, was Martin's second wife; they had three daughters and a son. But Alice's father also had four other children by his first wife. In December 1889, nearly a year after his father's death, William M. Nolan (son of Martin and his first wife) brought Alice's mother to court, contending that she was 'discontented with the shares which she and her family have got' and that 'the relations between the two branches [of the family] had been very strained since Testators death.' It seems almost certain that in 1889 Alice's mother was in no position to dower one of her daughters.[24]

Nora and Alice might have returned to Castleisland or stayed in Dublin, but for what purpose? There were few employment opportunities in either place. Marriage, of course, was always a possibility; however, not many educated women in the West eagerly chose it. Many of them feared 'a loveless marriage, hard work, poverty, a large family and often a husband who drank.'[25] Nora and Alice— and numerous others like them—entered religious life for a variety of reasons. All of them believed that they had a vocation, that God had called them to a life of service in the church. Yet there were other attractions as well. Teaching and nursing religious communities offered an exciting opportunity to young women of respectable families who had no career alternatives to marriage and motherhood. They provided such women with a setting in which to use their education, develop their talents, and assert a measure of independence. Not surprisingly, nineteenth-century Ireland saw a dramatic increase in the number of women entering convents.[26]

The day that Nora and Alice departed from Cabra was, no doubt, bittersweet. Both felt a certain amount of excitement accompanied by a great deal of sadness. Their leavetaking proved so difficult, in fact, that two days later their feelings hit rock bottom— victims as they were of 'seasickness, homesickness, heartsickness and any other kind of sickness you please.' However, during the long days at sea, Nora and Alice gradually recovered. They remained duty bound and even a bit anxious, particularly when their thoughts turned to New Orleans; but their daily jottings also show that they became quite carefree and adventuresome.

Indeed the purpose of Nora and Alice's diaries was to record their 'adventures.' Although we are not exactly sure who gave the notebooks to them—it was most likely Mother Prioress (who Nora mentions as having given them apples) or Sister Columba (who Alice says placed her in charge)—their instructions seem clear enough. Nora and Alice were expected to write about interesting sights or unusual experiences that occurred during their voyage. And once they reached New Orleans, they were to send their journals back to Cabra for the Sisters and the students to read.

Like the majority of diaries written in the nineteenth-century, Nora and Alice's notebooks were meant to be read. It is a modern, twentieth-century notion that diaries or journals record the secret, innermost thoughts and feelings of individuals. Women diarists of the eighteenth and nineteenth centuries often wrote as a way of keeping important family or community records of births, illnesses, marriages, deaths, visits, or unusual occurrences that made up so much of their daily lives.[27] Equally common were the journals of women migrants or emigrants that served as 'extended letters' to those left behind. These diaries, more than any others, were shaped by a sense of audience—one that informed the travellers' 'accounts of wondrous and unfamiliar sights and their efforts to come to grips with a new life.'[28]

Nora and Alice's diaries are 'natural,' spontaneous, and sincere. They are not introspective; yet they are revealing. Perhaps the most startling passages are those in which Nora and Alice describe their first impressions of the black people with whom they came in contact during stopovers at ports in the West Indies and on the decks of the *Floridian*. Nora and Alice may have been two of Cabra's best students, but their education had not prepared them for this encounter. Confused by what they saw and heard, they turned for instruction and advice to fellow-travellers and especially to the ship's captain.

Captain Sandrey was about fifty years old, weighed approximately eighteen stone, and came from Devonshire. Despite the fact that he was

English, he was 'by no means unreasonable,' according to Nora and Alice. They considered Captain Sandrey's ideas about the Irish and Home Rule 'very fair in most points'; and they genuinely enjoyed his company, especially his 'hearty laugh.' They also found him to be 'a capital storyteller' with a jolly, 'good-natured' face; and they felt privileged when he invited them into his quarters and allowed them to borrow his books. It was in the company of this genial and witty captain, who 'hate[d] the very sight of them [blacks],' that Nora and Alice formed their opinions about people of colour. For, until they arrived in the West Indies, it is highly unlikely that they had ever seen a black person.

The racial attitudes of Nora and Alice (and Captain Sandrey) are not surprising if one recalls the prevailing racism of the English-speaking world at that time. Even the most respectable opinion—and not simply popular intolerance—held that Africans were ineradicably inferior to whites; and since blacks (especially former slaves) appeared uncivilized in European terms, they were often considered 'savages.' It would be some years before anthropologists and other social scientists, led by Columbia University's Franz Boas, began seriously to question this 'scientific' racism.[29] Unfortunately, Nora and Alice's experiences on board the *Floridian* predisposed them for what they would find in New Orleans.

Despite its occupation by northern troops during most of the American Civil War, New Orleans remained a segregated society well into the twentieth century. Civil rights legislation passed in the years immediately following the war's end did little to change entrenched behavior; and during the 1890s new 'Jim Crow' laws would be passed to turn back what small improvements blacks had won. In 1890, for instance, the state of Louisiana required railroads to provide separate (and equal) accommodations for black and white passengers; and in 1898 a state constitutional convention mandated segregated schools. Not until the 1960s would white public and parochial schools open their doors to African-American children.[30]

Thousands of Irish emigrated to New Orleans during the antebellum period (before 1861), as they did in even larger numbers during the late nineteenth century. Poor, hungry, and in need of work, the Irish clashed regularly with blacks for the jobs on the docks and in the trades that nobody else wanted. The Irish won in the end, but not without creating intense feelings of hostility. As a result, later generations of New Orleans Irish 'inherited a blind and unreasonable hatred of the Negro.' [31]

The Catholic Church, which was mainly a church of immigrants throughout the nineteenth century, failed first to speak out against slavery and then to act in 'a unified and practical way' on behalf of emancipated African Americans. Although there are reasons that help explain these lapses, they nonetheless remain 'tragedies of American church history.'[32] Above all, the immigrant church lacked resources—money as well as priests, nuns, and brothers. Catholic leaders also felt a stronger commitment to assisting the impoverished Catholic immigrants who swelled their ranks than to aiding a more harassed and controversial group, especially when so few of them were Catholics. And, as a community of 'foreigners,' the church was badly crippled by the nativism that threatened it everywhere, including the Protestant South, where most blacks lived. Thus bishops and priests, who were conscious of the Catholic Church's minority status, remained cautious and generally allied themselves with white society. Nuns, too, were 'persons of *their* time, products of an environment in which racism was almost universal.'[33]

Young Irishwomen, like Nora and Alice, who journeyed out to America in the nineteenth century as religious women regarded themselves as 'missionaries.' However, those who went to cities like New Orleans and to Irish parishes like St John the Baptist—where Nora and Alice lived for the rest of their lives—ministered to predominantly Irish families that church leaders believed were in danger of losing their faith and in need of Catholic schooling. With great good will and few questions asked, nuns followed the the directives of their ecclesiastical superiors. Having vowed obedience, Sisters did not, as we might wish, 'speak out' or challenge accepted behavior.[34] Thus it seems safe to assume that Nora and Alice's racial attitudes did not change perceptibly once they became Sister Patricia and Sister Columba.

Whether they ever adapted to the 'oppressive' heat and humidity of New Orleans is not known. The Dominican Sisters at Cabra and Nora and Alice's families in Castleisland have not located any letters from them. But the first Irish Dominicans who came to New Orleans in 1860 found the summer sun 'scorching' and made some modifications—switching from heavy, wool serge inner-sleeves to cotton ones, for example—in their dress.[35] The majority definitely missed, as Nora and Alice probably did too, Ireland's cooler climate. And they did so for reasons of health as well as comfort.

New Orleans is located largely below sea level and has a semitropical climate. It is situated in a crescent-shaped bend on the lower Mississippi about 100 miles north of the Gulf of Mexico. Despite its distinction as a major commercial center during the nineteenth century, the Crescent City was also known for its undrained swamps and unsewered streets, making it the South's unhealthiest municipality. It earned its reputation as 'the graveyard of the Southwest' during the 1850s when yellow fever epidemics in 1853, 1854, 1855, and 1858 'brought a veritable reign of death.'[36]

Yellow fever is an infectious disease transmitted by the *Aedes aegypti* mosquito, which thrives throughout the year in tropical climates. Only during warm weather (but not every year) did the disease find its way into New Orleans, arriving on ships from places in Central America, Mexico, or the West Indies. Because the cause of yellow fever was not discovered until the early twentieth century and because its appearance was so haphazard, no one was ever certain when this southern scourge would attack—or how to prevent or limit its spread. The only certainties during the nineteenth century were that yellow fever hit towns and cities almost exclusively; most of its victims were newcomers or strangers; and people of colour resisted it better than native whites.[37]

The most devastating epidemic occurred in 1878.

It began in New Orleans and then spread quickly throughout the South and up the Mississippi Valley. Between July and November, yellow fever struck more than two hundred communities in eight states, causing a heavy loss of life (approximately 20,000 deaths) and major disruptions in international and local trade.[38] The epidemic's unusual severity provoked urgent demands for sanitary reform and stricter quarantine regulations. Following several years of conflict among public health agencies, commercial organisations and business groups, new quarantine facilities—an inspection station and mechanized equipment for the disinfection of vessels—finally went into operation in June 1885.[39]

The individual most responsible for these improvements was a native New Orleanian, Dr Joseph Holt, who was elected president of Louisiana's Board of Health in 1884. An expert in maritime sanitation, Holt believed that germs, not mosquitoes, were the culprits in the spread of yellow fever. He directed, therefore, that all vessels entering the port of New Orleans from 'yellow fever regions' be detained at least five days and, if infected, seven to ten days. During this quarantine period, 'every available part of a vessel, together with all the baggage and apparel of every person on board' was disinfected with bichloride of mercury, concentrated gas fumes of sulphurous acid, and exposure in an extremely hot steam-drying chamber.[40]

Although Nora and Alice seemed unacquainted with the reasons for the fumigation that took place on board the *Floridian*, they described its thoroughness well. There is little doubt that very soon they learned of yellow fever's tragic history and witnessed the fear that rumors of an outbreak could provoke. Communities of Irish nuns had not been spared when epidemics struck. In 1867 and 1878 all the Dominican Sisters had become infected; they were fortunate, however, in that only one newcomer died. The Mercy Sisters, who were not cloistered, mourned the loss of eight nuns to yellow fever. Their superior, Mother Austin Carroll, observed in 1880 that 'New Orleans lost more Mercies in twelve years than Cork had in forty.'[41]

Yellow fever was, undoubtedly, the big killer in New Orleans, but many individuals also died of consumption. Often considered a northern disease, tuberculosis took a great number of southern victims, particularly among the Irish. Since the incidence of tuberculosis was high in late-nineteenth-century Ireland, it was inevitable that many emigrants would carry infections with them. The fact that they chose to settle in urban areas and were often forced by their poverty to live in crowded and unsanitary surroundings meant that the disease continued to spread among them.[42]

Nora probably brought an infection with her, especially since both sisters who followed her to New Orleans also died of tuberculosis. However, it is likely that the difficult climate and the long hours she worked in one of the city's oldest and poorest Irish parishes, first as teacher and then as head mistress of St Mary's Academy, were not conducive to good health and long life. Yet, the year before Nora died, she—unlike Alice—returned to Ireland. In May 1906 Nora, now Sister Patricia, accompanied Sister Paul Campion on a recruitment trip. Not only did Nora have an opportunity to visit her family, but the two

Sisters also returned with thirteen eager and devout young women who wanted to become nuns in America. Among them was Maggie Prendiville, Nora's nineteen-year-old sister who had also attended Cabra. The circle was now complete.[43]

Alice, who also became a teacher in the same Irish parish, died suddenly (of carditis) in 1910, three years after Nora. Maggie (Sister Teresa) and Nell (Sister Gertrude) Prendiville fell to tuberculosis in 1927 and 1928. Another Prendiville sister, Sister Mary Austin (Kate), who wrote sadly from Nottingham, England, at Nell's death, hinted at her family's losing battle with tuberculosis: 'As for myself, I dare not cough. It seems to be the personal business of each one [in the convent] to take care of me.'

For the most part, Sister Austin's thoughts and prayers were with her sisters buried in 'dear old New Orleans.' She reminded the Mother Prioress to whom she wrote that the Prendivilles had long been connected to New Orleans, and she recalled how 'Columbus was not half as proud of his discovery of America as I was when as a child I found that dear old spot on the map.' She knew, however, that when Nell died 'the last link' with New Orleans was 'now severed'—except for her thoughts, which she promised would 'often fly to your little cemetery, where my three loved ones are.'[44]

Notes

1   Both girls were born and baptised in Castleisland, County Kerry: Honoria Prendiville was born on July 16 1868 to John and Julia Daley Prendiville at Gort Glass; and Alicia Joseph Nolan was born on March 19 1869 to Martin and Ellen Sullivan Nolan at

Droumtrasna. Birth and baptismal certificates can be found in the archives of the Dominican Sisters, Congregation of St Mary, New Orleans, Louisiana. The captain's name, Samuel S. Sandrey, appears on the *Floridian's* Passenger List Number 148 (October 14 1889), National Archives and Records Administration, Washington, D.C. I am grateful to Constance Potter, reference archivist, for helping me find this list.

2   Sister Mary Patricia Prendiville died on 20 May 1907 and Sister Mary Columba Nolan died on 18 December 1910. Sister Patricia, then headmistress of St Mary's Academy, was the subject of a long obituary in the *Daily Picayune-New Orleans* on 21 May 1907. Sister Columba received a shorter death notice on 19 December 1910. We learned that she was called 'Dovey' from a biographical sketch of Sister Mary Agnes 'Lambie' Gilmore, a friend of Sister Columba who also lived in the convent at Dryades Street. (The Latin words *columba* and *agnus* mean dove and lamb.) 'Sister Mary Agnes Gilmore, OP,' typed manuscript, Dominican Sisters' Archives, New Orleans.

3   Alice Nolan attended the Presentation Sisters' national school from 1876 to 1882; she was then a boarder at Cabra for four years, from 1885 to 1889. (Her two sisters, Ellie and Bridget, remained at Cabra at least through 1890.) Nora attended the same national school for two years longer than Alice, from 1876 to 1884; then in 1887 Nora entered the boarding school at Cabra but remained there for only two years. This information is contained in the 'Register of Presentation Convent National School,' Roll Number 6215, Parish: Castleisland 1876–84, Presentation Convent National School Records, Castleisland, County Kerry; and in the account book of 'Immaculata 1878–90,' Dominican Convent Archives, Cabra.

4   Hannah Prendiville, who was married to Nora's

youngest brother and who was alive in the summer of 1992 when Margaret MacCurtain and I visited the Prendivilles at Gort Glass, told us about the large Prendiville family. The current parish priest at Lixnaw sent me information on Alice's uncle and godfather, Father Thomas Nolan, in a July 1992 letter. And Sister Mary Vincent, OP, at Siena Convent in Drogheda confirmed what I learned about Alice's half-sister, Mary Julia, from jottings in the Nolan family Bible during my visit to Droumtrasna. Mary Julia had attended boarding school at Drogheda in 1879, entered the Dominican novitiate in 1883, and became Sister Mary Patrick in 1884. She died of influenza on 13 February 1924 at Drogheda. See 'Mother Mary Patrick Nolan 1924,' in 'Annals,' Siena Convent Archives, Drogheda, County Louth.

5   Rev Kieran O'Shea, *Castleisland: Church and People* (County Kerry: Kerryman Ltd. 1981), 23–8. Original prospectus entitled 'Boarding School under the Patronage of His Grace, the Most Rev. Dr Murray, at St Mary's Convent, Cabra, Dublin,' 1835, Dominican Convent Archives, Cabra. For more on the post-Famine rural bourgeoisie, see Emmet Larkin, 'Introduction' and 'Church, State, and Nation in Modern Ireland,' in *The Historical Dimensions of Irish Catholicism* (Washington, D.C.: Catholic University of America Press 1984), 8–9, 100–101.

6   *Ibid.* See too the Immaculata account book for the names and numbers of students in attendance during the late 1870s and 1880s. The penal legislation prevented both Catholics and Presbyterians from establishing their own schools.

7   *Freeman's Journal*, 1 July 1887.

8   'Boarding School...at St Mary's Convent, Cabra, Dublin.'

9   *Ibid.* See also 'St Mary's Dominican Convent, Cabra,

Boarding School, under the patronage of His Grace the Archbishop of Dublin,' *Irish Catholic Directory, Almanac and Registry* (Dublin: John Mullany 1885), 76. The same advertisement appeared in subsequent editions of the *Directory* during the late 1880s.

10 'Honour List: St Mary's Dominican Convent, Cabra,' 1885–9, Dominican Convent Archives, Cabra. See also a series of 'Programmes' for the same years. An 1892 newspaper clipping entitled 'Dominican Convent, Cabra. A Remarkable Entertainment,' written by 'a Visitor,' described an unusual exhibit on magnetism and electricity constructed and explained by 'a number of girl lecturers of ages varying from ten to eighteen.' On the significance of education to Irishwomen in the late nineteenth century, see David Fitzpatrick, '"A Share of the Honeycomb": Education, Emigration and Irishwomen,' *Continuity and Change*, I, No. 2 (1986).

11 The routine of the Cabra boarder, which changed little during the school's existence, was reconstructed by Sisters Terence O'Keeffe and Margaret MacCurtain, OP, from their own knowledge and from materials in the Dominican convent archives. I am very grateful to both of them.

12 'Boarding School...at St Mary's Convent, Cabra, Dublin.' For an understanding of the devotional revolution—of which retreats, novenas, and Forty Hours were a part—that took place in the Catholic Church between 1850 and 1875, see Emmet Larkin, 'The Devotional Revolution in Ireland 1850–75,' *American Historical Review*, 77 (June 1972), 625–52.

13 Former pupil of St Mary's to Mother Prioress, [n.d.] 1898, Dominican Convent Archives, Cabra. On the famous Maher and Cullen families, see Peadar Mac Suibhne, *Paul Cullen and His Contemporaries Vol. I: With Their Letters from 1820–1902* (Naas: Leinster Leader

Ltd. 1961), 184–5.

14 Suellen Hoy, 'The Journey Out: The Recruitment and Emigration of Irish Religious Women to the United States 1812–1914,' *Journal of Women's History* (forthcoming in 1994).

15 Sister Helen Nelon, OP, 'Narrative Account of the Dominican Congregation of St Mary, New Orleans,' Dominican Sisters' Archives, New Orleans; and Sister Mary Louise Albrecht, OP, 'Mother Mary John Flanagan, OP (1827–1904),' *Immaculata* [Cabra publication], II (1960), 16. This article was first published in *Salve Regina* [St Mary's Academy publication], XXVII (Jan. 1960), 6–13.

16 Religious communities established academies (boarding schools) 'to provide room and board for students who lived too far away to commute every day, to provide a formative Catholic environment for the education of youth, and to provide a source of income for the religious community itself.' Michael J. McNally, 'A Peculiar Institution: A History of Catholic Parish Life in the Southeast (1850–1980),' in Jay P. Dolan, ed., *The American Catholic Parish: A History from 1850 to the Present Vol. I: Northeast, Southeast, South Central* (New York: Paulist Press 1987), 170. See also *Portrait of Love 1860–1960* (New Orleans: Dominican Sisters, Congregation of St Mary 1960); Roger Baudier, *The Catholic Church in Louisiana* (New Orleans 1939), 393, 421; and James William Mobley, 'The Academy Movement in Louisiana,' *Louisiana Historical Quarterly*, XXX (July 1947), 953.

17 Charles E. Nolan, 'Modest and Humble Crosses: A History of Catholic Parishes in the South Central Region (1850–1984),' in Dolan, ed., *The American Catholic Parish*, 255–6; Baudier, *The Catholic Church in Louisiana*, 393, 461–3, 563; 'Mother Mary John Flanagan,' 17; and Nelon, 'Narrative Account of the

Dominican Congregation.'

18 Nelon, 'Narrative Account of the Dominican Congregation'; and 'Mother Mary John Flanagan,' 20.

19 Sister Barbara DuPuis, archivist of the Marianite Sisters of the Holy Cross in New Orleans, kindly provided this information; and Sister Margaret O'Brien, principal of the Presentation Sisters' school in Castleisland, graciously searched the student register for the names of Nora Quilter and Mary Twomey. The *Floridian's* passenger list, already cited, recorded the names of the entire party that travelled from Dublin to New Orleans.

20 From the birth and baptismal certificates in the Dominican Sisters' Archives in New Orleans, we know that Mary Twomey was born at Knockane, a townland close to Droumtrasna, in Castleisland; and that Mary Mahon was born in Rathfarnham, a suburb of Dublin. Mary Twomey, although a good deal younger than Nora and Alice, attended the same national school (from 1879–1887) as they did. From a letter quoted in Nelon, 'Narrative Account of the Dominican Congregation,' we also know that Mary Twomey had a relative at Cabra who was a professed Sister and that Mary Mahon was a niece of Cabra's Sister Martha. Despite the fact that Mary Twomey's name does not appear in the boarding school account book or on any honours lists at Cabra, it does appear on a list of 'Postulants and Novices who Went from Cabra to New Orleans,' Dominican Convent Archives, Cabra. The original list, however, was sent in 1985 by Sister Helen Nelon, OP, archivist in New Orleans, to Sister Bertranda Flynn, OP, archivist at Cabra.

21 Hoy, 'The Journey Out.' In writing that essay I benefited greatly from the important work of two historians, the first Irish and the second American. See especially the book and essays by Caitriona Clear:

46

Nuns in Nineteenth-Century Ireland (Dublin: Gill and Macmillan 1987); 'The Limits of Female Autonomy: Nuns in Nineteenth-Century Ireland,' in Maria Luddy and Cliona Murphy, eds., *Women Surviving: Studies in Irish Women's History in the 19th and 20th Centuries* (Dublin: Poolbeg 1990); and 'Walls within Walls: Nuns in Nineteenth-Century Ireland' in Chris Curtin, Pauline Jackson, and Barbara O'Connor, eds., *Gender in Irish Society* (Galway: Galway University Press 1987). See also articles by Margaret Susan Thompson: 'Sisterhood and Power: Class, Culture, and Ethnicity in the American Convent,' *Colby Library Quarterly*, 25 (Sept. 1989), but recently updated and published as 'Cultural Conundrum: Sisters, Ethnicity, and the Adaptation of American Catholicism,' *Mid-America*, 74 (Oct. 1992); 'Philemon's Dilemma: Nuns and the Black Community in Nineteenth-Century America: Some Findings,' *Records of the American Catholic Historical Society of Philadelphia*, 96 (1986); and 'Women, Feminism, and the New Religious History: Catholic Sisters as a Case Study,' in Philip R. Vandermeer and Robert P. Swierenga, *Belief and Behavior: Essays in the New Religious History* (New Brunswick, N.J.: Rutgers University Press 1991).

22 'List of Dowries 1843–57' at the end of the St Mary's Convent Account Book, Dominican Convent Archives, Cabra. The other sisters who accompanied Mother Mary John Flanagan to New Orleans in 1860 had dowries that ranged from £150 to £800.

23 Hannah Prendiville and her son, Bernard, told me about the large Prendiville family and showed me several photos of the nuns (Nora, Kate, and Maggie) in their family. Later, at the Dominican Sisters' Archives in New Orleans, I saw documents indicating that Nell and Maggie had followed Nora to New Orleans and had become Sisters Gertrude and Teresa.

24   I first learned of Martin Nolan's death (January 20 1889) at the cemetery located at the end of Chapel Lane in Castleisland. Rev Thomas Nolan PP Lixnaw, erected a marker in memory of his brothers. When I later visited the Nolans at Droumtrasna they gave me a copy of the 'Solicitors' Notes,' December 14 1889, in the case of William M. Nolan. These 'Notes' described the two families of Martin Nolan; and the quotation in the text is taken from this document.

25   Mary Carbery, *The Farm by Lough Gur: The Story of Mary Fogarty* (Cork: Mercier Press 1986 paperback ed.), 47. See too Mary Feeney's view in Liam O'Flaherty's 'Going into Exile': 'Her mother's life loomed up before her eyes, a life of continual misery and suffering, hard work, birth pangs, sickness and again hard work and hunger and anxiety.' Liam O'Flaherty, 'Going into Exile,' in Seamus Deane *et al*, eds., *The Field Day Anthology of Irish Writing, Vol. III* (Derry 1992), 120.

26   From 122 nuns in 1800, the number rose to 1,552 in 1850, and to 8,031 in 1901; in 1800 the ratio of nuns to Irish population was about one per 32,000, but in 1900 it grew to approximately one per 400. See Hoy, 'The Journey Out.' See also J. J. Lee, 'Women and the Church since the Famine,' in Margaret MacCurtain and Donnacha O Corrain, eds., *Women in Irish Society: The Historical Dimension* (Westport, Conn.: Greenwood Press 1979), 37–45; Clear, 'Women in Nineteenth-Century Ireland,' the first chapter in *Nuns in Nineteenth-Century Ireland* 1–35; and David Fitzpatrick, 'Marriage in Post-Famine Ireland,' in Art Cosgrove, ed., *Marriage in Ireland* (Dublin: College Press 1985), 116–31.

27   On the significance of diaries, Thomas Mallon remarked: 'These aren't just books that were written; they're books that happened.' Thomas Mallon, *A Book*

of One's Own: People and Their Diaries (New York: Ticknor & Fields 1984), xviii. My understanding of nineteenth-century diaries has been expanded by the following: Suzanne L. Bunkers, 'Diaries: Public and Private Records of Women's Lives,' *Legacy,* 7 (Fall 1990), 17–26; Margo Culley, ed., 'Introduction,' in *A Day at a Time: The Diary Literature of American Women from 1764 to the Present* (New York: The Feminist Press 1978), 3–26; Arthur Ponsonby, ed., 'Introduction on Diary Writing,' in *English Diaries: A Review of English Diaries from the Sixteenth to the Twentieth Century* (London: Methuen & Co. Ltd. 1922), 1–43; and Penelope Franklin, ed., 'Introduction,' in *Private Pages: Diaries of American Women 1830s–1870s* (New York: Ballantine Books 1986), xiii–xxvii. Finally, I credit my interest in diaries to the Pulitzer Prize-winning book by Laurel Thatcher Ulrich, *A Midwife's Tale: The Life of Martha Ballard, Based on Her Diary 1785–1812* (New York: Vintage Books 1991).

28 Culley, 'Introduction' in *A Day at a Time,* 8.

29 The best study on this subject is John S. Haller, *Outcasts from Evolution: Scientific Attitudes of Racial Inferiority 1859–1900* (Urbana: University of Illinois Press 1971).

30 Mary Lee Muller, 'New Orleans Public School Desegregation,' *Louisiana History,* XVII (Winter 1976), 80–81 (on Catholic schools); John W. Blassingame, *Black New Orleans 1860–1880* (Chicago: University of Chicago Press 1973), 217; and Eric Arnesen, *Waterfront Workers of New Orleans: Race, Class, and Politics 1863–1923* (New York: Oxford University Press 1991), 88–89.

31 Earl F. Niehaus, *The Irish in New Orleans 1800–1860* (Baton Rouge: Louisiana State University Press 1965), 49–54 (quotation appears on p. 51). See too Randall M. Miller, 'A Church in Cultural Captivity: Some

Speculations on Catholic Identity in the Old South,' in Randall M. Miller and Jon L. Wakelyn, eds., *Catholics in the Old South: Essays on Church and Culture* (Macon, Georgia: Mercer University Press 1983), 36–38.

32 Cyprian Davis, OSB, *The History of Black Catholics in the United States* (New York: Crossroad 1991), 116, 121.

33 Randall M. Miller, 'The Failed Mission: The Catholic Church and Black Catholics in the Old South,' in Miller and Wakelyn, eds., *Catholics in the Old South, 155–6, 169*; and Thompson, 'Philemon's Dilemma: Nuns and the Black Community,' 7, 13–14 (quotation). Nineteenth-century nativism in the United States favored the interests of indigenous inhabitants over immigrants.

34 *Ibid*, 13. On religious as missionaries, see Edmund M. Hogan, *The Irish Missionary Movement: A Historical Survey 1830–1980* (Dublin: Gill and Macmillan 1990) 14–16; and on Catholic schooling, see Jay P. Dolan, *The American Catholic Experience: A History from Colonial Times to the Present* (New York: Doubleday and Company 1985), 263–93.

35 Sister Xavier Gaynor wrote in 1912 that she had spent 'fifty years under the scorching sun of N.O.' Sister Xavier Gaynor to Mother M. Bertrand Maher, Feb. 17 1912, Dominican Convent Archives, Cabra; and Nelon, 'Narrative Account of the Dominican Congregation.'

36 John H. Ellis, *Yellow Fever & Public Health in the New South* (Lexington: University Press of Kentucky 1992), 32; and James O. Breeden, 'Joseph Jones and Public Health in the New South,' *Louisiana History*, XXXII (Fall 1991), 341–42.

37 Jo Ann Carrigan, 'Yellow Fever: Scourge of the South,' in Todd L. Savitt and James Harvey Young, eds., *Disease and Distinctiveness in the American South* (Knoxville: University of Tennessee Press 1988), 57–9;

and Ellis, *Yellow Fever & Public Health*, 31.

38 *Ibid*, 56.

39 *Ibid*. See the chapter on 'The New Orleans Sanitary Association' (pages 83–104), and especially those pages (100–101) on the new quarantine facilities and service. See too Breeden, 'Joseph Jones and Public Health,' 358–9. In 1884 the Louisiana Supreme Court upheld 'the legality of state quarantine fees as a legitimate exercise of the state's police powers to protect the health of its citizens.'

40 Joseph Holt, 'The Sanitary Protection of New Orleans, Municipal and Maritime,' in *Public Health: Papers and Reports of the American Public Health Association*, XI (1885), 93–5. See also 'The Louisiana Quarantine on the Mississippi River,' *Mississippi Valley Medical Monthly*, VII (June 1887), 273–4; and Joy J. Jackson, *New Orleans in the Gilded Age: Politics and Urban Progress 1880–1896* (Baton Rouge: Louisiana State University Press 1969), 175–77.

41 Sister Mary Hermenia Muldrey, RSM, *Abounding in Mercy: Mother Austin Carroll* (New Orleans: Habersham 1988), 155, 197.

42 Ellis, *Yellow Fever & Public Health*, 29; Leonard G. Wilson, 'The Rise and Fall of Tuberculosis in Minnesota: The Role of Infection,' *Bulletin of the History of Medicine*, 66 (Spring 1992), 18, 24–5; and David M. Emmons, *The Butte Irish: Class and Ethnicity in an American Mining Town 1875–1925* (Urbana: University of Illinois Press 1989), 72–5.

43 In an unpublished history of the New Orleans Dominicans (Congregation of St Mary), Katherine Burton in 1959 described the recruitment trip to Ireland in 1906. (Katherine Burton, 'Women of Valor,' in Dominican Sisters' Archives, New Orleans). In her account of Sister Patricia's death in 1907, Burton says she was 'Mistress of Schools' (principal) at St Mary's

Academy on Dryades Street. The records of this boarding school seem not to exist. The school and the convent were torn down to make way for a state highway; however, St John the Baptist Church remains standing.

44 Sister M. Austin to Mother Prioress, 11 Feb. 1929, Dominican Sisters' Archives, New Orleans. Kate Prendiville entered the Sisters of Saint Joseph of Peace (the religious community founded by Margaret Anna Cusack, better known as the Nun of Kenmare) in July 1901 and lived in that community until her death in January 1960. As Sister Austin, she taught in St Augustine's School, Nottingham, from 1901 to 1912 and spent some of 1912 and 1913 at St Mary's Training College, Southhampton. In 1913 Sister Austin was appointed headmistress at St Mary's School, Hyson Green, and remained there until she retired in 1950. I am grateful to Sister Patricia, CSJP, archivist at the Sacred House Provincial House, Leicester, for this information.

PART II

NORA'S DIARY

September–October 1889

Written on board the Steam Ship Floridian, *en route from Liverpool to New Orleans, length 360 feet, breadth 41, depth 27 d[itt]o. Owned by West India & Pacific S[team]. Ship Company Limited.*[1]

> Adieu, Adieu, my native shore fades o'er the
> waters blue,
> The night winds sigh, the breakers roar,
> And shrieks the wild sea-mew.
> You sun that sets upon the sea, we follow in his
> flight,
> Farewell awhile to him and thee.
> My native land—Good night.[2]

I do not intend, dear reader, to preface these notes with any remarks as to my feeling on the eventful evening we set out from dear St Mary's to cross the dark, deep sea, never more to revisit the shores of green Erin. To give you even a faint idea of what they were, would, I feel, not be an easy task, besides I have promised that this should be a quite natural diary and as such I propose it for your perusal.

Wednesday 11 September
It was a beautiful calm evening on the date above

mentioned, when our party embarked on board the little boat which should convey us to Liverpool. We started at 9 p.m. and for a considerable time watched, in silence, the apparently receding lights of the city, for it was quite dark and we could not see land. When the last had faded from our sight we agreed to go down, and feeling in good form for supper, adjourned to the saloon. We had just ordered a very substantial one, when at that very inopportune moment I felt the first symptoms of seasickness. At first I thought it was only [my] imagination, and tried to battle with it, but I had to give in. Of course my companions only laughed at me, but I soon had the satisfaction (if so I may call it) to see them all sick after supper. It was agreed on all hands that we should retire to bed which we accordingly did. I, dreadfully sick as I thought, while in reality I did not know what seasickness was till the following day. A few hours later we were awakened from a refreshing slumber, and pleasing dreams, by a series of sounds of no assuring kind. On enquiry we ascertained that the paddle box had given way. This did not make a very serious impression on me (as I often told you my spirits are very elastic) so I asked in what part of the world we were, and at what time we would be likely to leave it. As an answer to my first, the stewardess surmised that we were a little past Skerries;[3] to my second I received the *comforting* assurance that we might not start until Thursday afternoon. Under these circumstances we tried to sleep again but in vain. However at 8 a.m. the *Cavan* was again gaily riding the waves but not for long, and by a half hour's fitful sailing after a few hours anchorage alternately, we expected to make up for lost time. To add to our discomfiture it leaked out somehow that the captain himself did not know where we were, and that the *Cavan* had drifted ten miles out of its course. The elements too seemed to be against us for we were completely enveloped in a dense fog, so dense that we barely avoided running into another boat which was only five yards ahead. And, you may ask, what were the thoughts that coursed through our minds during all this time. Why, Miss Flanagan was seasick for fully five minutes at the idea of being late for the *Floridian*. As for myself—what with the machinery giving way half a dozen times, our drifting to some unknown region, the constant fear of running ashore or anything else equally extraordinary—after a little deliberation I came to the conclusion that we should never arrive at our destination. However 'Life at most is but a span, always make the best of it,' as Alice used to quote and so we tried, and the result answered our expectations. At 4 p.m. the *Cavan* was progressing favourably under such circumstances and we had the consolation of knowing that we were nearer Liverpool than when we started. Boats were continually passing us on their way to the spot we had left. It seemed so long ago, and of course we gratified our curiosity by reading the name of each. After this distressing occupation I was just going off into dreamland when I heard a little commotion beside me. I looked up and there before me lay a large ship with the name *Floridian* painted on it 'as large as life.' For the moment I could scarcely believe my eyes and in that instant I thought all hope was over and that we were too late. But a welcome message from the *Floridian* greeted our ears. It said that the captain would kindly wait, and receive us on board at 8 p.m. He had moved down the Mersey in hopes of seeing us and had almost given us up in despair when we put in an appearance. Things having begun to brighten up a little, Alice and I thought we would let you know if we were still over water and we accordingly did so, substituting the bench for a desk and the deck for a seat. At 5 o'clock we were overtaken by the *Leitrim*, which had been sent out to meet us some hours before by the officials of the company, but which we had missed in the fog.[4] Our delay occasioned them great anxiety which increased to alarm on seeing some logs of timber floating about in the Mersey. After explaining the cause of our delay our boat was taken in tow by the *Leitrim* and was gliding smoothly along for nearly two minutes when the rope broke. So, dear reader, you see everything was against us. Again the *Cavan* showed an unmistakable desire for going backwards instead of forwards, for just in sight of the docks it drifted back five miles with the tide. But if I go on telling of all our mishaps I shall never arrive at the Prince's Dock,[5] which we eventually did, and it was no small relief to our party to find themselves standing once more on *terra firma*. But not for long were we allowed to enjoy that pleasure, as the company had ordered a tender to be in readiness to convey us to the *Floridian*. A few arrangements having been made relative to our luggage we embarked on the *Iron King*, to retrace our way down the Mersey accompanied by a few of the officials who made provisions against our not reaching the ship in due time. The bare possibility of our being late created great anxiety, for we had no other alternative but to remain a week or ten days in Liverpool; and that to a party of weary heartsick travellers, such as we were, would be disagreeable in the extreme. Fortunately such was not to be, and it was with much satisfaction, and many fervent *Deo Gratias,* we perceived the lights of the big ship gleaming in the darkness. In a few minutes we were safely transferred to our cabins, Alice and I in one, and the remainder of the party in an adjoining cabin. Having deposited our small parcels and taken off our wraps, we repaired to a very substantial supper of tea and cold meats and did such ample justice to it, as only hungry travellers can (for you will please remember we had had nothing to eat since the previous evening). And now, dear reader, you will naturally suppose I should sensibly retire for the night which I intend to do immediately as I feel, well I cannot exactly tell you how I feel. It is a combination of seasickness, homesickness, heartsickness and any other kind of sickness you please, so I shall say good night.

Friday 13

Made a rather serious mistake this morning for which there was but one remedy. Alice was awake first and having looked at the watch ordered me out of bed saying I would be late for breakfast. Why, I was in such a hurry getting out, I forgot to open my eyes and consequently nearly knocked my head off against the bed post. I then got myself into my clothes as quickly as possible (my eyes not yet open) expecting to hear the breakfast bell every moment. At last I did manage, somehow, to get my orbs sufficiently open to see the watch when lo! and behold! it was only ten past seven instead of ten past eight. And now the question arose, 'How shall we get through the hour?' At 8.30 we were summoned to the saloon,[6] where a tempting breakfast was laid including various dishes of meat (notwithstanding it is Friday) but our party were too exhausted to indulge in anything except a cup of tea, which, by the way, is not as unpalatable as I had anticipated. Here I had an opportunity of seeing all my fellow travellers, as the *Floridian* has no accommodation for steerage passengers. They are ten in number not including the captain and officers, three of whom sit at table with us.[7] As the captain does the honours I shall do him the honour of describing him first. But how? Well, I can only say he has the jolliest, most good-natured face you ever saw, and is ready for a joke at any moment. At his left sits a bonnie Scotchwoman and at his right, the most pious looking of our sex on board, 'A minister's wife.' The former is going to visit a brother in Jamaica, the latter to Jamaica also, with what purpose I have not heard but it is probably to assist her husband, who is also on board, in the *conversion* of the natives. Then there is an Englishman whom I should not know to be such, though I sit beside him, but for a few remarks the jolly old captain passed regarding Ireland's right to Home Rule.[8] Oh! if you could only see how he fumed and stormed! Happily it occurred at dinner at which I was not present else the storm might have broken unmercifully over my head, for I should have enjoyed myself, I fear at his expense. I don't think the captain will broach that subject again. Alice sits next me and her neighbour I recognised as a Frenchman by his bonjour and extreme partiality for sweet things. I often wondered why Alice did not engage him in conversation, but I have come to the conclusion that her humility could not stand the shock that a betrayal of her knowledge of 'the languages' might expose her. On the opposite side next his countrywoman sits a Scotchman, a resident in New Orleans for thirty years but who has been home to see 'his dear ould counthry' and is now returning to America. Then the minister's family, four in all, including the nurse, and not forgetting the squalling baby who has found the use of his tongue at 4 o'clock in the morning. Breakfast over, we agreed to take a walk on deck, and really our attempts at walking were simply ludicrous. Luncheon time came on, 1 p.m., and we obeyed the summons to it rather reluctantly; but, Oh! such a calamity. I had just got through a few morsels when I had to renew an acquaintance with that old sea monster. Early this morning we 'fairly descried land, whether the Kerry or Wicklow mountains we could not tell, but they lay very high.' However the captain soon came to our assistance, and informing us they were the latter, bade us take a last farewell look at green Erin not knowing what a more powerful attraction the former had for us. So I employed the remainder of the day in watching those receding mountain tops grow dimmer and dimmer, till the falling shades of night hid them completely from my view. My *unwelcome guest* is determined to keep a strict watch over me for the present and will not allow late hours. So gentle reader I shall now say good night.

Saturday 14
Rose at 7.30, and Alice and I had a good half hour's

walk on deck before breakfast, which was considerably enlivened by a chat with the minister and his wife. We agreed with them that it was a beautiful morning, and that we had a very calm sea. But when Mr Picot, assisted by his better half, began to discuss with us the good that priests might effect if assisted by a wife, and even went so far as to tell us he had heard some priests say so we disagreed entirely with them, and told them so, at the same time kindly reminding them they would scarcely succeed in converting us; and they wisely took the hint and decamped. That dose was quite enough—breakfast, luncheon, dinner, and tea to us today. Indeed if he says any more on the subject I will be tempted to give him some of my mind, but he looks as if he ha[s] common sense.[9] There is nothing else interesting to speak about except the passing ships which we soon lose sight of, and the huge porpoises or pig fish we occasionally see following the ship.[10]

Sunday 15

Sunday in St Mary's, and Sunday on the broad Atlantic. I shall not make a digression on either, dear reader. I feel it would be a fruitless attempt to show you what the latter is like. Though the sea is as smooth as glass, and the sky a beautiful azure flecked here and there with fleecy clouds, there is a depression on the spirits of all I could readily account for. Even at table nobody felt inclined to talk. Perhaps they were too busily engaged otherwise, but I think if I had been there I should have found time to say even, 'Pass the bread, please.' And so the day has passed without anything interesting having occurred.

Monday 16

I awoke this morning to find myself partly out of bed without the trouble of getting out. My first prayer was a fervent *Deo Gratias* that I was not in a higher bunk else I should have come to grief, I fear. Such heaving and such rolling even though there is scarcely a ripple on the calm sea. I put in an appearance at breakfast, dinner, and tea today, as the captain said something about throwing me overboard if I mutinied any more. Besides I have said a long good bye to my *devoted friend* (the seasickness) with a hint that I shall not require his companionship any longer. But really I do hate sitting there at table with nobody saying anything. Of course Alice and I try to keep up a conversation between ourselves, but the result is that I am treated as Sancho Panza was by the doctor.[11] For no sooner had I commenced to talk than my delicious hot soup was whisked away, not by a conjuring stick but by a hand from behind, before I had scarcely tasted it. Well, he shall go without the spoon next time, as I intend to keep peaceful possession of that till I am quite finished that course. Our chief amusement today consisted in watching the vessel cutting its way through the blue waves. Indeed we spent most of our time in this fashion. Though the sea is quite placid looking, the ship is rolling considerably owing to a groundswell. I intend to place a buttress against my bunk, in case I too might think of rolling about.

Tuesday 17

Rose at 6.30 and found it was a beautiful morning though a little hazy. I was surprised to hear the foghorn a little after 8 a.m. But my surprise was nothing in comparison with the captain's; he was lying on the sofa awaiting the summons to breakfast when the unwelcome signal greeted his ears. In an instant he was on his legs and in the next nearly fell over a poor sailor (which would be of no small consequence to that individual, the impending weight being only about eighteen stone) in his hurry to ascertain if the ship were on fire; but no, we had only been suddenly enveloped in a thick fog which cleared away after a few hours. The remainder of the day was beautifully fine. As usual the conversation flagged at dinner but I do not wonder now, why. Unless he spoke about the weather, the poor captain could not broach any other subject without fear of giving offence. We have such a combination of nations on board, English, French, Scotch and last though not least Irish, which has the largest number of representatives. The weather is becoming a little warmer and the evenings unpleasantly short. In fact there is no evening, the night falls so quickly.

Wednesday 18

> Two poor young ladies aweary
> Tired not of work but of play,
> Put to each other the query,
> How shall we get through the day?

I cannot tell what possessed us to come without needlework. However I do not see why we should fret so much about that as long as 'we have leave to speak.'12 While taking our usual walk before breakfast the captain told us we passed west of the Azores at 2.30 this morning, at a distance of three miles. Had

not the *Cavan* met with so many mishaps we should
have seen them in the daytime. We have a lovely
calm sea and a cloudless sky. The sunset too was
magnificent beyond description. So enchanted were
we with the beauty of the scene before us that we
almost forgot where we were. The tea bell soon put
an end to our reverie and we went down 'just to
oblige the captain.' I am getting a most ferocious
appetite. That performance over we decided to have
a good walk before 'turning in for the night.' Really
the Heavens now presented an appearance it would
be utterly impossible for me to describe. Perhaps
there is no necessity though, as, I suppose my
'learned friend' has already done so in her notes. It
was long before we thought of retiring to rest. Indeed
I could have stayed on deck all night. We sighted a
sailing vessel in the evening, but it was too far distant
to be recognized. Nothing else of importance
occurred to break the monotony today.

Thursday 19
How I really managed to get out of bed this morning
is a mystery to me still. Why, I am sure I was not fully
awake when I came on deck at 6.30. Whether it was
the constellations last night [that] had such an effect I
cannot tell; but of course I am the 'junior' and am not
at liberty to question Co[mpany].'s authority, but I do
hope she will not rise so early or cause me to do so
any more.[13] The morning was beautifully fine; there
was scarcely a ripple on the calm sea, save where the
waves divide at either side and these are crested with
snowy foam. It is so beautiful. Alice and I have the
deck all to ourselves before breakfast every morning,
and we were particularly glad of that this morning as

we had an opportunity of rehearsing all the little incidents that happened since this day week. Only a week away from Cabra! It seems to me as if the days were months. After breakfast we were looking about for some kind of work when I espied a little parcel in the corner of my workbasket. I opened it and found it contained materials for making *Agnus Deis*. [14] Such a welcome discovery. Thank God we need not be idle now for some time. The day passed more quickly and pleasantly than any yet for we are now quite at home on the sea, but a serious loss which I sustained tended to make it rather unpleasant for me. Alice and I were leaning over the railing eating a few of the apples which M[other]. Prioress had so kindly given us.[15] I had a delicious one and had just finished peeling it when in the act of taking the first bite it fell overboard, and the worst of it was it was the last in our possession. Until then I never realized the truth of the proverb that says 'There is many a slip 'twixt the cup and the lip'[16]; however I had to join in the laugh against me and make the best of a bad matter. The sunset this evening was not as beautiful as last evening's, and the sky was not as clear. We remained in the saloon after supper and indulged in a few games of draughts. The steward and stewardess are very obliging and let us have any games we require.

Friday 20

Following S[ister]. M[ary]. Catherine's advice,[17] we took some lessons early this morning from one of the officers; we have been doing so during the past week on a smaller scale. Now we are learning the use of the various instruments we see. I must admit we sometimes look, after a quarter of an hour's catechising as if our instructor had been talking Greek. But as he is very patient and good humoured, he laughs as much at our mistakes as we do ourselves. I hope you too, dear reader, will be a little considerate and remember that 'we are at sea' in more senses of the phrase than one. We are now in the Sargasso Sea, as we discovered by a species of moss, which is thrown up by the Gulf of Mexico, and is seen drifting about here.[18] Kind Heaven treated us to a very rare amusement this afternoon, the pleasure of running from a shower of rain. We were standing under shelter of a boat when it commenced and thought it would be only a mist, but it was quite the contrary and compelled us to beat a hasty retreat. I need not say we enjoyed the sport immensely. You would scarcely believe what a source of pleasure the slightest incident is on board. The day was beautifully fine except for that one shower. After dinner we sighted a sailing vessel bound for Liverpool. The captain communicated with it by means of letters and ascertained that it was a French vessel that had not seen land for three months, and in all probability will not for another month either. It is very interesting to watch their manner of saluting the different ships we meet. The sky last night was quite clear and studded with brilliant stars. Really it was magnificent. Alice and I were looking out for the different constellations. The former is quite proud of her position when I remind her she is taking S[ister]. M[ary]. Columba's place here,[19] with this difference—that the pupils of the latter are seniors while I am as *my mistress* says a 'junior.' A long and pleasant chat with the captain contributed also to our enjoyment of the scene. He is a capital storyteller, and entertained us for fully two hours relating his nautical adventures and hair-breadth escapes. Among other subjects he spoke of the great risks incurred by the captains and officials of fast sailing vessels. This led us to speak of the number of Irish emigrants, and then somehow I found myself suddenly in the middle of a political discussion. The captain, though an Englishman, is by no means unreasonable. On the contrary his views regarding Home Rule are very lenient. I think he enjoyed the chat as much as we did, if I could judge by his hearty laugh when we related some little incidents that occurred during the agitation. Well, but we really had presumption. Perhaps the other ladies sitting down below thought so too. However, it was the captain [who] came to us, therefore we were not to blame. Being very tired and sleepy too, I shall now say good night.

Saturday 21
Rose at 5.30 ship time. Alice persists in keeping Cabra time which is two and a half hours faster. The difference between the two was the cause of no small amount of amusement at breakfast; for instead of half past 8 it was 11 o'clock by her watch. The sky is as usual cloudless, and its deep azure reflected on the calm sea beneath gives the latter a beautiful appearance. The heat was rather oppressive and, but for a few refreshing showers of rain accompanied by a slight breeze, I would not feel at all certain that we might not evaporate or be decomposed into something extraordinary. But speaking of a cloudless sky, and then rain, might seem inconsistent but such is really the case. In less time than it would take to tell you, the rain comes on and just as quickly the sky

becomes clear again. It is surprising to see with what alacrity the waiters secure the ventilators and port holes; it is much better though to watch that performance from a distance, else you would stand the risk of being *run over*. We saw a beautiful rainbow this afternoon. It spanned the Heavens and its reflection on the water was simply magnificent; the tints were so deep and distinct. I have rarely seen such a beautiful one. We have not forgotten that this is Ember Week.[20] However Miss Flanagan and N[ora]. Quilter's memories were, to all appearances, very treacherous at dinner for they helped themselves to a sausage roll apiece. I am Miss Flanagan's vis-à-vis, and all but succeeded in choking myself with fright lest she should eat it. So it was with no small amount of satisfaction [that] I heard the waiter remind her that it was a fast day. N[ora]. Q[uilter]. had by this time got through some of hers. She too was quickly brought to her senses. I firmly believe she has scruples about it yet, which we did not endeavour to remove. I don't know how we all keep from laughing though when she speaks about it. By this time you are quite as tired of this day's uninteresting diary as I am myself, and if so, that is quite enough. I hope our stay in St Thomas will enable me to tell you something interesting. As it is, comparatively nothing happens to break the monotony of our sea life.

Sunday 22

Alice and I treated ourselves to a good swim before breakfast this morning.[21] As we had no other means of changing the routine we took advantage of that. How shall we get through the day, seemed to be the uppermost thought in everybody's mind at breakfast. For, even though it is a gorgeous morning today, nobody (barring Alice and myself) seems to enjoy it. We played draughts for a considerable time during the day at which the whole Picot family were shocked. Young Master and Miss Picot, aged seven and five respectively, very charitably reminded me that it was sinful to do so on Sunday. At first I had a mind to send him about his business, but on second consideration I told him we were capable of judging for ourselves. Still he persisted in his endeavours to dissuade us from it, his sister chiming in occasionally with 'Pa says so.' Then Alice informed them that their creed and ours were different; and I wound up the discourse by telling them that we were much obliged for their solicitude about us, but that their further interference was not required. I am inclined to think they consider reading on Sundays sinful also. For though the passengers usually spend the day reading, not one except the Englishman has opened a book. The conversation at dinner was very much enlivened by the captain's anecdotes of his home life and a dispute he had also with Mrs Picot respecting the size and number of the streets in Port-au-Prince, her native place. The former persisted in saying there was but one, while the latter boasted of half a doz[en]. It reminded me so much of similar discussions in Cabra regarding a little place in the province of Munster.[22] The heat is becoming daily more oppressive, and a few showers this afternoon were a welcome boon as they tended to cool the atmosphere considerably. Except while at table we spent the entire day and even part of the night on deck. What would I not give, were it possible to bring the pupils of the Immaculata and nuns too out here for the afternoon recreation. Of course we should then invite them to stay for tea, which would give them an opportunity of seeing what a starlight night is on the ocean. But we must be content with witnessing that scene ourselves and leave the aforesaid pupils to their peaceful enjoyments on *terra firma*.

Wednesday 25

Land in sight! This welcome news was announced outside our cabin this morning by one of the officers. We had our toilet partly completed, and indeed, it did not take us long to put the finishing touches to it. We came on deck immediately and there a welcome surprise awaited us, for almost beside us to the left lay a long range of hills. The nearest part looked barren and devoid of vegetation of any kind; but as we proceeded further on, Nature seemed to be more generous, and shrubs and evergreens covered the steep declines. On our right lay a little Spanish town of no great importance save for its lighthouse and mines of phosphorous.[23] While in the dim distance we could see Dog Island boldly outlined against the clear, blue sky.[24] We did not lose sight of land during the entire day (you can imagine what a treat that was to us, who had not been favoured with such a sight for the past fortnight), and at 3 p.m. we perceived the little town of St Thomas partly hidden by the surrounding hills. As we came nearer its beauty unfolded itself more plainly to our view. As for me, I was lost in admiration of the scene before me. The town is situated in a little valley surrounded on three sides by hills covered with shrubs and evergreens.

The houses are built in Danish style and are surrounded by balconies. At first sight they appear to be very closely built together, and rising in stages behind one another.[25] The former impression is removed when you walk through the streets (which by the way are not anything half as grand as the *New Lime*),[26] but in the latter case appearance is a reality. So that approaching it as we did from the sea, we could see almost every house in it before setting foot on shore. To approach it by any other way would be rather dangerous, for had you missed your footing you would undoubtedly find yourself deposited rather unceremoniously on a house top, or perhaps fall[ing] down through a chimney. But how stupid. I have not yet told you how many of us went to explore the, to us, unknown region. Of course I shall give the Parson and his wife the first places and 'Moonseer,' Miss Flanagan, Alice, and I completed the party. It was only two minutes before the boat started [that] we made up our minds to go, and poor Miss Flanagan had given us up in despair. To tell the truth, I had some dire forebodings as to whether I would return as sound as when setting out, not knowing what species of humanity we might fall in with. But a few specimens in the form of boatmen and officials allayed my fears. We had leave of absence for an hour and a half, and during that time I saw at least three white men and one woman. All the other inhabitants were not exactly black, though darker than copper colour. The costume worn is white, even the gentlemen are dressed in white. Well, if we weren't stared at. If we *wanted notice* anyhow, we got plenty of it. The first place we directed our steps to was the Catholic Church. Really I never felt such a thrill of joy as I felt on finding myself once again in presence of the Blessed Sacrament.[27] It is a lovely building, though small and is dedicated to St Thomas. There are two other altars besides the principal altar, one dedicated to Our Lady and I do not know to whom the other is dedicated. The former was being decorated for some feast or devotions by a few ladies and one of the priests of whom there are two. Germans, I believe. Their dress is not unlike the Vincentians, but I did not hear to what order they belong. The little church shows every sign of being well kept; it is scrupulously clean. There are no galleries except the organ gallery. Indeed I was rather surprised to see that instrument in such an apparently poor place. The people were very kind and gave us all the information we required. After leaving the church we strolled through the other parts of the town. The streets though narrow are clean; the houses I have already described. We had a good opportunity of criticising the inhabitants; and they, apparently, went on the same plan themselves. The men are very industrious looking, at least there are no idlers lounging about. I wish I could say the same for the women. For the most part, they have a very slovenly appearance, caused I suppose by the oppressive heat. Some you would meet walking about with trays of very uninviting cakes and sugarsticks on their heads; others [were] sitting basking in the shade indulging in a little gossip. We visited some shops to try and procure large sun hats (I hope this won't lead you to imagine we are tawnies. Oh no! Not yet!), but the prices were fabulously high. The pursar had occasion to buy a few yards of braid and actually paid 1/6 for what he would get for 2d in England or Ireland.[28] It was such a curiosity and he got such a 'take in' that he showed it to us. That will give you an idea of their exorbitant prices, though the town is free of duty. We returned to our ship at 5 p.m. delighted with the adventures of the last hour and a half. I have told you the town, as I saw it in the daylight, was beautiful looking; but as seen from the deck after tea it was still more beautiful. The hills cast a deep shadow over it, so that you could see nothing but the lights like so many stars glimmering in the darkness. It was like fairyland. I shall never forget it. We stayed looking at the scene until near 12 o'c and very reluctantly we retired even at that hour. Several passengers have come on board during the evening, but I could not spare them a look. I had to spare them my ears though to hear a few youngsters crying and whining. Even at this hour one of them is enlivening the scene with its *sweet strains*. It is now near one o'clock, and very probably Alice will insist on my turning out of bed at six in the morning. So I shall say good night.

Thursday 26

The events of this morning fully justified my fears of last night, though Alice was not the delinquent; but a young monkey not able to walk, who kept up an incessant bawling from about three till six this morning. Then the note was taken up by four or five others on deck; somebody told us they were singing. For my part I did not know what to make of the unearthly noise, however I determined on seeing as soon as possible. Arrived on deck, I there beheld a real gypsy encampment. A party of thirteen females, including the children, squatted on mats under the awning or lounging on deck chairs. I confess my first impressions were not of the nature I should like, and I fear my last will correspond with them. Their appearance is simply revolting and anything like decency seems to be quite foreign to them. Some of them are almost hideous looking and have enormous mouths extending from ear to ear. The captain said of one of them that, when he laughs, half his head's off. At breakfast I saw the remainder of the party in the form of a minister, a doctor, and another gentleman who seems to be nothing in particular. These last are far more civilised looking than the women. If we could judge by the amount of jewellery some of them wear they seem to be immensely wealthy. Even the first mentioned individual is adorned with a pair of lovely gold earrings. The captain did not expect so many passengers yesterday but the election of a President in Port-au-Prince necessitated their removal to St Thomas, and they are now returning.[29] I believe, when a disturbance occurs in any of those islands, as many as conveniently can, remove to the adjacent islands till the storm blows over, and then return. Excepting the Scotchman, our fellow travellers (including the late addition) will part with us in a few days so that we shall have the entire place to ourselves. We feel lonely already at the idea of parting with some of them. But we spent a most enjoyable day notwithstanding, looking at our coloured neighbours and listening to the captain's witty remarks. He hates the very sight of them. I sincerely hope they will be merciful tonight, though, and not frighten us out of our wits with their cackling. Fortunately none of the juveniles are near Alice and myself.

Friday 27

The sight of land this morning was not much of a novelty, though one feels in better spirits on beholding it. The land now lying before us is San Domingo; as we go farther on, it gets the name of Haiti.[30] It is very hilly country and well wooded. In some parts enormous grey rocks are to be seen, also deep ravines down the sides. On the whole it is not very desolate looking, though animal life in any shape or form we could not see even when nearest. Later on in the day we perceived smoke rising behind one of the hills; this led us to the conclusions that there must be a village or town there. This was the first island Columbus discovered on his route to the western world.[31] It is said to be as large as Ireland, and a beautiful country in the interior. None of the niggers were indisposed save one who felt 'a bit nasty.' It would not be such an awful calamity if a few of the ragamuffins' tongues felt so. Why, the strength of their lungs is marvellous. As Alice and I were walking after luncheon, in despair almost at having nothing to read, the captain invited us into his sitting room. This is such a *sanctum sanctorum*,[32] and it is such a great privilege to be allowed [to] enter it that all thoughts of what might be his object in asking us in went clean out of my brain. His next move was to open a well filled bookcase, and invite us to select from it as many books as we wished. Wasn't it very kind of him, and didn't we tell him so; indeed if we never said a word he could have read gratitude in our looks. At about 6 p.m. we were much startled by some vivid flashes of lightning. At first we did not notice it much, but the flashes becoming more frequent we thought it safe to retire. Mr Evans (the

Englishman) quieted our fears by telling [us] it was harmless to the ship. It is a peculiar kind of forked lightning and is frequently seen in those parts. The sunset was magnificent; this is the only adjective I can apply with fitness, and still I feel it will not convey to you its indescribable beauty. The sunlight was succeeded by a glorious moonlight which lasted but for a few hours.

Saturday 28

This morning we lay at anchor before the little town of Gonaïves.[33] It is not near as pretty looking as St Thomas. In fact, the latter is superior to it in every respect. There was not much accommodation for our going ashore, but the few who have been there told us we were not much at a loss for not having seen it. Part of the cargo consisting of four enormous boats was unloaded here. It took an immense lot of time and trouble to get them out, besides there was great responsibility in the undertaking as the price paid for their carriage (£600) shows. We were confined to the saloon or the smoking room during the greater part of the day as they were unloading coal also, and the dust was flying uncomfortably in all directions. I was made fully aware of this fact after a little business was done in that line, by somebody mistaking me for a nigger. You know I am determined to keep my original colour at least till I reach New Orleans. So that mistake stimulated me to go down and see if I would recognize myself. If there was any person else in the cabin at the time I should find a little difficulty in doing so; however I took it for granted that it was myself till I got my face clean. When we could persuade ourselves to appear again on deck it was after tea; and we amused ourselves by watching the lightning which continued after we retired, for we could see it flashing by the port holes. In the meantime a party of eight refugees came on board our vessel from a German steamer. Their transfer was the cause of great alarm both to themselves and the captain; for in crossing from one ship to the other, they might have been pursued and captured by the inhabitants, which would lead to fatal results. The blacks resemble each other so strongly that they got mixed up before I had an opportunity of seeing them. Indeed the whole party in general furnish us with much cause for amusement.

Sunday 29
The unloading of the cargo not having been completed we are still at anchor. The coaling business was resumed early this morning and we were prisoners downstairs until evening, even then we did not venture up till the deck was washed. However the time did not pass unpleasantly. Alice and I made use of the opportunity to write our diaries; during the evening we had a nice view of the island. It is very pretty in some places where the hills slope gently and shut in on three sides a little valley covered with shrubs and evergreens. On the whole the scenery is very attractive. At 6.30 p.m. we again set sail and expect to be in Port-au-Prince in the morning.

Monday 30
Our expectations were fully realised and at an early hour. This morning we anchored before the little town of Port-au-Prince. I confess I was a little

disappointed in its appearance, having heard so much about it from Mr and Mrs Picot; but every person likes to stand up for his own country and Mr Picot firmly believes it ranks next to Paris in importance. It is prettily situated on the slope of a hill and in former times was rather a large and important place. But in one of the revolutions, which are frequent here, a great part of the town was totally destroyed; even now we can see the ruins. Some of the houses have been rebuilt, but they say it will be long before it regains its former position. The surrounding country is hilly and richly wooded; beyond those hills it is fertile and very productive. We got some oranges just plucked from the trees, also bananas, sugar cane and pears. Mr and Mrs Picot went ashore; but we had scarcely time to feel lonely, when a party of seventy niggers came on board to console us for their loss. The ship was literally besieged by applicants who wanted to go to Kingston[34] and the result is 'that of niggers we can offer a charming variety.' Why, there is not a square inch of the deck bare; they are so thickly squatted around. How I wish they were gone! We have had such a pleasant voyage since the first week (you know I am passionately fond of the sea now) that a party of blacks breaking in on our enjoyment is disagreeable in the extreme. I don't know why I have taken such an utter dislike to them, but really their appearance alone excites disgust. Our stay here was shorter than I expected and at 5 p.m. we again set sail. The captain thinks we will be in Jérémie early in the morning. We had a long chat with him after tea, and he gave us some idea of the state of government and management of the natives of the different islands. He says they are little more than cannibals, those with whose presence we are now blessed included. So that if you happen to hear of my mysterious disappearance some fine morning, you may rightly conjecture what has become of me. However it is to be hoped we shall be soon rid of them.

Tuesday 1

The sight of human habitations is such a usual thing, that the little town of Jérémie[35] was not much of a diversion this morning. We were made cognisant of our whereabouts early enough by a dozen or so of boatmen who had come out to the ship to take any passengers, who so wished, ashore. Our cabin is just under the gangway, so that it was *exceedingly comfortable* to hear a dozen fellows bawling almost into our ears before we were rightly awake. It wouldn't have been so bad if I understood what they were saying, but I fear S[ister]. M[ary]. Vincent[36] will be quite ashamed of her pupil when she hears I could not translate a syllable of their French. Jérémie is not at all an ugly little town, though at the same time, it has not much pretension to beauty. The chief feature is its situation. The houses show very well being built on a slope and the thickly wooded hills form a pretty background. On the whole the scenery is very picturesque. We had a pretty long time to look about, as it takes a good length to unload forty or fifty tons of cargo. We set out again at 3 p.m. None of the passengers went ashore. We had been on the lookout for the past few weeks for sharks; we were very curious to see one and quite unexpectedly our curiosity was gratified. A little before dinner the captain told us there was one in the neighbourhood. I need not say we were all eyes till we saw it. It was six feet in length; any more I cannot tell you though, as that gentleman was too modest to appear above water save for that once. We saw some pelicans here also. The sunset these evenings are magnificent. I have never seen anything like them. And then such glorious moonlight. How often I have wished that the inmates of St Mary's could share this pleasure with us. We stay on deck till eleven and twelve o'clock sometimes, and even then find it hard to go down.

Wednesday 2

Though Jacmel was not mentioned in the list of ports at which we were to call, the captain was obliged to do so having to deliver some cargo there. He would much prefer to avoid it as the anchorage is very unsafe; in fact, it is one of the most insecure ports in the West Indies.[37] We arrived at 6.30 a.m. The sun was so powerful even at this early hour that we could not distinctly see it for a long time. The houses are larger than in Jérémie. It is a very disinteresting little place. A few of the niggers went ashore for half an hour or so. The country around is much the same as in Port-au-Prince and Jérémie. We started again at 3 p.m. and, though reluctant to leave the other ports, were glad to get away from this. Only a few yards distant we could see a steamer which had been wrecked a short time ago. It has lain in the same position ever since the accident occurred. The blacks have been pretty quiet all day save for an occasional whining among the juveniles. We are looking forward with the greatest anxiety for their departure.

Indeed I am sure I shall be inconsolable tomorrow. Though so far from St Mary's, our thoughts were centered there this evening for we could not forget the children's retreat. One of my first observations regarding it to Alice was about the difference in the temperature. This time last year I was very nearly frozen to death, while now I am not at all sure that I shall not come to that end by being baked. We are going into retreat too. I wonder shall we keep it.

Thursday 3

'Narrow escape from drowning.' It is usual with us to leave the ports open at night as well as in the daytime to get as much air as we can. But last night we got rain as well, more than we bargained for. One of the ports is directly over my bunk. The rain came directly through it, therefore, I got a delicious shower bath about two o'clock in the morning. It had been trickling down my face for fully ten minutes before I felt it, so that my hair was wringing wet when I awoke. I fear I had not many scruples about breaking 'the retreat' (which I kept remarkably well since I got into bed) and the only consolation I received from my companion was a peal of laughter. My next move was to get a towel to wipe my face; and before that process was completed I was fast asleep, at least so I concluded from finding the towel [a]round my head in the morning. It must have been very agreeable for the blacks to get their faces washed too with so little trouble. I expected to find them floating around on deck, but to my surprise they were as spruce as you please in white and print calico dresses. This is the 'going home day for them.' We sighted the coast of Jamaica at an early hour, and at 8 a.m. could see

Kingston and Port Royal in the distance. At ten
o'clock we anchored outside the latter; not having
any cargo we did not touch the shore. It is customary
for vessels bound for Kingston to call at Port Royal,
as the passengers must be examined by a doctor
before they are allowed to proceed. We were exempt
from this ordeal, but I dare say it is before us yet. The
delay was only for half an hour, and at 10.30 we put
into Kingston. Did I ever dream when the capital of
Jamaica was being drummed into my head that I
should ever set foot on its shore. The company have a
wharf so that we can do so as often as we like. After
seeing the niggers off and squeezing out a few tears
after them, we took a walk through the town. We
kept to the principal street and this led us to 'the
gardens,' a very cool, pretty little place. After indulging in a few minutes rest we proceeded to the
Catholic church which is only a little distance from
them. I need not tell you what our emotions were on
finding ourselves in the presence of the B[lessed]
Sacrament again. The church was pretty well filled
and confessions were being heard, so we had no
opportunity of seeing much of it. In the meantime
Miss Flanagan went to visit the Sisters of the
Immaculate Conception, and obtained permission for
us to be present in their little church for four o'clock
Benediction.[38] What bliss! You must have had
Benediction about the same time too. We are some
three or four hours slow. Here also we had not much
opportunity for looking around as we were expected
to be back to dinner at 5 p.m. There are twelve nuns
in all, dressed in the Franciscan habit.[39] Their little
church, though small, is pretty and neat. The singing,
though, was most atrocious. We were obliged to

direct our steps homeward after leaving this, but Alice and I intend to have a glorious day of sightseeing tomorrow. The town is very quiet, much quieter than you expect one peopled with half-savages to be. The moonlight is glorious. We can see the country around as distinctly as in broad daylight.

Friday 4

After breakfast Alice and I set out on our expedition. We had the entire day at our disposal and intended to make the most of it. The first objects of interest were the streets, which are pretty wide. The walks are very rugged though, so that we had to divide our attention between walking and sightseeing. I did not think the town was so extensive till I travelled through it. The stores too are very large. The sun was very powerful so we retired into the shade of the cool gardens after a few hours walking, and here we had luncheon under one of the shady bananas. The fountain and pond in the centre of the gardens are very pretty; the surface of the water is almost hidden by water lilies and other flowers. Here also we saw a variety of trees, with whose names we were already acquainted. Breadfruit tree. Cocoanut. African oil palm. Date palm. Casuarina, Eucalyptus, etc. etc. The cactus grows wild; in some places we saw hedges of it. There is also a variety of flowers, not now in bloom. About one o'clock we visited the Catholic church. Here indeed a pleasant surprise awaited us, for being the first Friday of the month there was Exposition of the Blessed Sacrament;[40] and truly it was an edifying sight to see the number of devout worshippers present there. We did not forget the nuns and children. Are we not very fortunate & at such a time too. Of course we could not go through the church, as we intended to; from what I could see it is large and well kept. There are handsome statues of the Sacred Heart, St Joseph, the B[lessed]. Virgin, and even St Patrick himself.[41] The altar was simply and nicely decorated for the occasion. I believe there is a good number of Catholics in Kingston. After having seen the ins and outs, lanes and streets of the capital, even to the Jewish Synagogue and Protestant church, we took a long drive in the country. I was under the impression when leaving Ireland that I should never see anything like its verdure again, but really Jamaica surpassed it in that respect. We drove through roads and lanes lined on either side with trees whose branches interlaced overhead, formed in some places regular arches. Occasionally we caught glimpses of mountains in the distance. The highest point is St Catherine's Peak, 5000 feet;[42] and the English soldiers camp is directly under it on another peak 4000 f[ee]t high. We passed by some lovely villas (in this country they are called 'penns')[43] with verdant lawns in front. Some little cottages are completely secluded in a network of flowers and creeping plants. The black soldiers' camp is situated a few miles outside of the town; they have a very extensive place. I have no idea of their numbers though. After driving around the place we returned by a different road to the town. I could not tell you how much we enjoyed the drive. Everything looked so fresh and pleasant in the cool evening. At home we were agreeably surprised to find our cabin half filled with cocoanuts. Mr Evans, the English gentleman, had called in our absence and kindly brought them, also some grapes and oranges. Miss

Flanagan and the others met him as they were going out. The evening was deliciously cool; the moon rose at six o'clock. It is gibbous with us, but I imagine it is far more brilliant than at home; I suppose because the sky is so clear. The men worked by its light, during the greater part of the night, unloading the cargo. It is amusing and interesting to watch them do so. It is now eleven o'clock, and as I am very tired after our day's adventures I shall say good night.

Wednesday 9

With your permission, dear reader, I shall pass over the events of the past few days and bring you without a word of preparation from the Gulf of Mexico, twenty miles up the Mississippi. There are several stations up the river, at a few of which the ships call. The first of these we reached at six o'clock this morning. Immediately a doctor came on board to see if there was any infectious disease among the passengers or crew. Not finding any, he gave us permission to proceed farther up the river to the second station sixty miles from N[ew]. Orleans. This is called 'quarantine.' Here the ship and its belongings had to undergo the process of fumigation. Palliasses, pillows, carpets, everything in the shape of cloth had to be taken out and hung on racks prepared for the purpose; these racks are so constructed as to be easily drawn between large cylinders. Inside these cylinders are tubes through which the fumes of sulphur and some chlorides are sent; the temperature being about 120 deg[rees]. The clothes are left for three quarters of an hour and are then withdrawn. After a few minutes airing, they are again ready for use. If it were only the things belonging to the ship that had to be fumigated it would not matter much; but every individual on it had to send his clothes, even those he never wore, to be fumigated also. It was with no good grace we unpacked our trunks, but it had to be done. There was no shirking it. When this was done, we were ordered to change our clothes and send them through the same process. Even our trunks and shoes were sprinkled with some purifying fluid. If you could see us at four o'clock as busy as bees rehearsing the scene of the 10 September. In the meantime the saloon, cabins, etc. were sprinkled with sulphurous water, and pans of sulphur were passed into the holds. This business commences in May and continues till November, and for every ship that is fumigated the company has to pay 160 dollars. This money goes to the state and, I confess, it is an easy way of making money.[44] We cannot leave here for five days, but the captain thinks he may obtain permission for us to leave on Sunday morning. We received some visitors this evening in the form of mosquitoes; they introduced themselves, and were evidently delighted to see us from the pertinacity with which they cling. They intend to escort us in triumph to New Orleans, and I suppose they will remain till they see us quite settled down in our new home.

And now, dear reader, as I have come to my journey's end,[45] and the end of my diary too, I shall return you my most sincere thanks for having read it through, if you have done so. I must also beg you not to criticise it too severely. I have done my very best to make it interesting, and if I have failed in this respect 'tis nature's fault,' not mine. But if I have been so happy as to succeed, it will be ample recompense for the trouble I have taken to know that it has added to your pleasure, and helped you to remember for a little time

A former pupil of St Mary's.

Finis

Notes

1   The *Floridian*, built in Belfast by Harland and Wolff, was launched on April 12 1884 and completed on August 16 1884. T. McCluskie (Technical Services/ Administration, Harland and Wolff) to Suellen Hoy, 26 Nov. 1992. The West India and Pacific Steam Ship Company, along with the Harrison and Leyland lines, dominated the Liverpool–New Orleans trade in the 1890s. In 1900 the West India and Pacific and the Leyland lines merged and, in the following year, were purchased by J. P. Morgan, United States railroad magnate. Eric Arnesen, *Waterfront Workers of New Orleans: Race, Class, and Politics 1863–1923* (New York: Oxford University Press 1991), 162.

2   From Lord Byron's 'Childe Harold.' See Lord Byron, *Childe Harolde and Other Poems* (New York: D. Appleton and Company 1899), 7.

3   The Skerries are the rocks at the northwest corner of Anglesey in Wales.

4   The *Cavan* and *Leitrim* were paddle-steamers built at Birkenhead in the 1870s for the City of Dublin Steam Packet Company, one of the first (and one of the most successful) of nineteenth-century steamship companies. The paddles that drove these ships (replaced in the 1890s by screw propeller-driven ships) were situated on either side of the ship in 'boxes' to protect the wooden paddles that revolved on an axis. Heavy seas quite frequently smashed the boxes and consequently laid the paddles open to damage. In this instance, one set of paddles had given

away and the other set was working against the considerable Liverpool ebb tide. The *Cavan*, only 275 feet long, was replaced in 1896 by a screw steamer that was twelve feet longer and seven feet wider. The City of Dublin Company was Irish-owned and largely crewed by Irish; although on the Holyhead route, for which it held all the records, crews were chiefly Welsh. John de Courcy Ireland to Margaret MacCurtain, O.P., April 5 1993.

5 Prince's Dock on the Mersey River was completed in 1821. The entrance was modernised in 1868. Francis E. Hyde, *Liverpool and the Mersey: An Economic History of a Port 1700–1970* (Newton Abbot: David and Charles 1971), 77. The Mersey River flows westward to the Irish Sea at Liverpool.

6 A 'saloon' is 'the officers' dining and social room on a cargo ship.' For all definitions, I have used the third edition of *The American Heritage Dictionary of the English Language* (Boston: Houghton Mifflin Company 1992).

7 Nora is mistaken, and Alice is correct. There are sixteen passengers: Margaret Flanagan, Nora Prendiville, Alice Nolan, Nora Quilter, Mary Twomey, and Mary Mahon; Mr and Mrs T. R. Picot and their three children and the children's nurse; Mr Evans, the Englishman, mentioned by name in the diaries; William McBride, the Scot, whose name appears on the *Floridian's* Passenger List; and finally two persons who remain nameless—the Frenchman and Scottish woman who, like the Englishman, depart before New Orleans.

8 The Irish struggle for self-government or legislative indpendence from England.

9 The minister is the Rev T. R. Picot (as noted in Alice's diary) who resided at Port-au-Prince. He is a Wesleyan Methodist, the oldest Protestant denomination in Haiti. Pastors were supplied from either

England or Jamaica. Rev Picot succeeded the Rev M. B. Bird, who had been pastor for over forty years. Pan American Union, *Haiti* (Washington, D.C.: Bureau of the American Republics, Bulletin No. 62 1892), 36.

10 Porpoises, which characteristically have blunt snouts, are sometimes called 'sea hogs' or 'sea pigs.'

11 In Cervantes's *Don Quixote*, Sancho Panza was encouraged to eat only a little by Doctor Rezio Tirteafuera. The doctor believed that this kind of diet, or fasting, sharpened the mind. Miguel de Cervantes Saavedra (1547–1616) is best known for this satirical and chivalric novel, which was probably read in parts at Cabra.

12 Nora seems to believe that they should enjoy this period of freedom. Once they officially enter the Dominicans as postulants, they will be obedient and abide by the long periods of silence.

13 At Cabra, boarders were very conscious of the distinction between 'juniors' and 'seniors.' The latter refers to the young women who had been at boarding school for the longest period of time. Nora was a year older than Alice, but Alice was definitely the 'Cabra girl.' She had been there two years longer than Nora; thus Alice was placed in charge. There are several references in the diaries to this arrangement.

14 Heart-shaped, stuffed satchels that were blessed and hung on the cribs or beds of babies and small children to protect them from sudden death or evil.

15 The Mother Prioress at Cabra from 1887 to 1893 was Sister Catherine de Ricci Maher, referred to in the introductory essay.

16 An ancient proverb, sometimes attributed to Homer. See John Bartlett, *Familiar Quotations* (Boston: Little, Brown and Company 14th ed. 1968), 311.

17 Sister Mary Catherine Murphy was one of Nora and Alice's teachers at Cabra.

18 The Sargasso Sea is a part of the northern Atlantic, located between the West Indies and the Azores. It is 'relatively calm' and 'noted for the abundance of gulfweed floating on its surface.' See *American Heritage Dictionary.*

19 Sister Mary Columba McDonnell was a teacher and friend to both young women. However, she seems to have had a special relationship with Alice, who would become Sister Mary Columba in New Orleans. Sister Mary Columba McDonnell was born in Carlow in 1857 and was, like Mother de Ricci, a member of the well-known Cullen and Maher families. In 1889 Sister Mary Columba was thirty-two years old.

20 Several days of fasting observed on Wednesday, Friday, and Saturday after the First Sunday of Lent, after Whitsunday, after September 14, and after December 13.

21 According to Alice, they took baths before breakfast.

22 She is referring to Castleisland, located in County Kerry and the province of Munster.

23 Sombrero, an island of St Christopher-Nevis in the Leeward Islands of the West Indies.

24 Tiny island between St Thomas and St John in the Virgin Islands.

25 St Thomas is not a town but an island of the Virgin Islands. Although settled by the Dutch, it later became Danish and remained so until 1917 when the United States acquired it. The town on St Thomas Island, and capital of the Virgin Islands, is Charlotte Amalie.

26 A walkway at Cabra on which the boarders strolled nearly every day.

27 The consecrated host in the Roman Catholic Church.

28 One shilling and sixpence versus twopence.

29 For the first nine months of 1889, there were riots throughout Haiti while the forces of General Florville Hyppolite and General Séide Thélémaque fought over

who would be the next president. During this time, Haitians fled in large numbers to St Thomas and elsewhere; finally in September, many felt comfortable in returning to Port-au-Prince and other parts of Haiti. General Hyppolite had won and became president until 1896. Robert I. Rotberg with Christopher K. Clague, *Haiti: The Politics of Squalor* (Boston: Houghton Mifflin Company 1971), 95–96, 98.

30 San or Santo Domingo is the capital of the Dominican Republic; Haiti shares the island of Hispaniola with the Dominican Republic. Port-au-Prince is the capital of Haiti.

31 Columbus claimed Hispaniola for Spain in 1492. Columbus's first discovery, however, was an island in the Bahamas.

32 The *American Heritage Dictionary* defines 'sanctum sanctorum' as 'an inviolably private place.'

33 A city of western Haiti situated on an arm of the Caribbean Sea.

34 The capital of Jamaica.

35 Another Haitian town, like Gonaïves, known for its exports of coffee and cacao.

36 Sister Mary Vincent Hogan taught French at Cabra.

37 This Haitian town is located on the southern coast 'at the extremity of a bay whose waters are very frequently boisterous.' Pan American Union, *Haiti*, 59.

38 A short service consisting of prayers, hymns, and a blessing of the congregation with a consecrated host.

39 At the Convent of the Immaculate Conception on Duke Street, the Sisters of the Third Order of St Francis staffed a boarding school that their community had established in Kingston in 1858. Joseph C. Ford and Frank Cundall, *The Handbook of Jamaica for 1919* (Kingston: Government Printing Office 1919), 377–78.

40 A popular devotion among Roman Catholics in which

a monstrance, containing a consecrated host, was exposed for several hours on the first Friday of each month.

41 Most Irish missionaries went to America and Australia during the nineteenth century, but in 1849 sixty-one Irish priests served in the Caribbean. Some came from diocesan seminaries (especially Ardagh and Kilmore); others were Redemptorists and Dominicans. But the majority were sent out from All Hallows. It had supplied forty-two priests by 1896. Edmund H. Hogan, *The Irish Missionary Movement: A Historical Survey 1830–1980* (Dublin: Gill and Macmillan 1990), 16, 45.

42 St Catherine's Peak is outside Kingston near Newcastle in the Parish of St Catherine. I thank Richard Blackett, Department of History, Indiana University at Bloomington, for sending me a map that indicates the exact location of St Catherine's.

43 Nora is mistaken. 'Penns' are not villas or estates; they are livestock farms that have been important to the island's economy since slave days.

44 Probably the captain's view—and that of the owner of West India and Pacific Steam Ship Company. The right to charge fees to underwrite the cost of the quarantine system was the result of a major confrontation between the State of Louisiana and powerful commercial and business interests. The state first authorised the collection of fees in 1874, but this decision was opposed by the Louisiana and Texas Railroad and Steamship Company. In 1884 the Louisiana Supreme Court reversed the ruling of a district court which had decided in favor of the railroad and steamship company. Finally in 1886 the United States Supreme Court affirmed the decision of the Louisiana Supreme Court. James O. Breeden, 'Joseph Jones and Public Health in the New South,'

the Louisiana Supreme Court. James O. Breeden, 'Joseph Jones and Public Health in the New South,' *Louisiana History*, XXXII (Fall 1991), 359.

45 On October 15 1889 Nora, Alice, and the two Marys officially entered the Dominican Sisters, Congregation of St Mary's.

ALICE'S DIARY

September–October 1889

Our route from Cabra to New Orleans. On board the
Floridian *built in Belfast in 1884 by Harland and Wolff
builders. Gross tonnage 3257 tons. Length 360 feet.
Breadth 41. Depth 27 feet. Horse power 1518. Crew all
hands: forty-four. Owned by West India and Pacific Steam
Ship Company Ltd, The Temple, Dale Street, Liverpool,
England.*

I fear it would prove a fruitless endeavour did I
venture to describe my feelings at leaving dear old
Cabra that hallowed spot where I spent so many
days and years of happiness and undisturbed peace.
I shall leave it to those who may read these notes to
picture how they should feel when about to bid
farewell forever to their much cherished and deeply
loved school-home which, from the happiness and
peace enjoyed within its walls, becomes in time more
endeared to them than their own family home. I do
not for a moment wish my readers to imagine that all
my days at school were spent in sunshine. Being a
daughter of Eve[1] I too had my faults and follies, not
trifling in number, but which continued corrections
and punishment made me mend little by little.

But, thank God, I sincerely hope these corrections

were not given in vain and that his Divine Grace has at last fallen on a fertile spot where I trust with its daily increasing strength it will bring forth a good harvest. Thanks also to my dear Mother Prioress and the dear good Sisters who have been so interested in me since I was given into their charge. May they increasingly reap success in their undertakings and may all who have ever been committed to their faithful trust prove a credit to St Mary's.

It would undoubtedly prove an endless task were I to enumerate the many reasons why I should leave my school-home feeling that I have there contracted a heavy debt of gratitude. But those who may glance [at] these notes will assuredly feel as I do that the only means I have of repaying that debt is by faithfully discharging the duties laid out for me in the path which I am now about to tread. By so doing I will prove myself to be what I most earnestly wish to be. A faithful child of St Mary's. And now that it has come to my turn to bid it 'Adieu' forever, it is not difficult to imagine how my heart should be almost torn asunder when bidding my long and last parting farewells. My only sustenance in this heartfelt struggle being the conviction that a high duty calls me hence. Yet I feel that as the years rapidly pass by and when leisure from the duties in which I am daily engrossed allows me some moments for reflection, it is with much pleasure and satisfaction [that] my thoughts will wander back to the happy days spent in St Mary's.

Wednesday 11/Thursday 12

At about half past four the cabs drove up which were to take us to the North Wall[2] where we were to

Exterior of Cabra (in 1909), the boarding school outside Dublin
that Nora and Alice remembered with such fondness

The Dominican Sisters at Cabra, to whom the diaries were also
directed. Front row, centre: Mother Prioress, Mother Catherine de
Ricci Maher; front row, end at right: Sister Columba McDonnell

The audience—young women and girls at Cabra in 1890—for
whom the diaries were written

Dublin's North Wall (c. 1890s), from where Nora and Alice departed for Liverpool
Courtesy of National Library of Ireland, Lawrence Collection

Where Nora and Alice, as Sisters Patricia and Columba, spent their lives in New Orleans (on Dryades Street). Centre, St John the Baptist church; right, St Mary's Academy and Convent; left, parochial school

Sister Patricia Prendiville, headmistress of St Mary's Academy, New Orleans

embark on board the *Cavan* for Liverpool.

After having bid a fond farewell to our revered Mother Prioress, our dear Sisters in Christ, and our loving companions we drove off and arrived at our destination about twenty to six. Making there a few necessary arrangements, shortly after six we went on board the little steamer which to our exceeding great joy and satisfaction did not start as soon as we expected. While waiting there we were entertained by ballad singers who rendered some very plaintive airs just suitable for such an occasion. Amongst them was: 'He'll be Back By and By.' This was quite out of place in our case, I trust.[3] Still the air was so plaintive and the scene so touching we were much moved.

At 8.30 our vessel set sail and as it slowly rent its way through the foaming waves we watched for the last glimpse of our dear and cherished fatherland which we hope never again to see. Oh then what feelings of grief and emotion filled our breasts when in the dim distance and darkness its green shores soon faded from our sight and left us to indulge in its view only in imagination.

> As slow our ship her foamy track against the
>   wind was cleaving,
> Her trembling pennant still looked back to that
>   dear isle twas leaving,
> So loth to part from all we love from all the
>   links that bind us,
> So trow our hearts as on we now to those we've
>   left behind us.[4]

Shortly after 9 o'clock we adjourned to the saloon to order supper and were just seated at table waiting to be served when Nora P[rendiville] was taken suddenly ill. Without waiting a doctor's opinion we concluded immediately it was seasickness. To my demerits, I fear it must be acknowledged, I laughed heartily at first but I soon got cause to regret my merriment, for in a short time after supper (of which Nora did not partake) the remainder of us were attacked with the like disease. We got into the berths as quickly as possible and very soon found ourselves in the arms of Morpheus wandering in the land of dreams.[5] At about 2 o'clock we were wakened by a terrific noise and on inquiring were informed the paddle box had given way and the steamer was at a standstill. On further inquiry, we heard the captain didn't know where we were situated but thought we [could] be only a little distance outside the Skerries.

Under these disheartening circumstances we tried to sleep again being both sick and tired. In the morning about seven o'clock we still found ourselves at anchor and ascertained it may be far in the day before we could resume our journey. This indeed was very unpleasant news to us knowing that our steamer, the *Floridian*, would start from Liverpool at 1 p.m. Were we late the consequences would undoubtedly be that we should remain in Liverpool for some time and wait the next steamer on the line, greatly to our regret as we had no fancy for being knocked about in an English hotel and were not much disposed for sightseeing. Our boat set sail again at 8 a.m. and came to a standstill at various intervals during the day. When we did not arrive in due time at the Prince's Dock, Liverpool, the company became alarmed and sent a few boats to our assistance. A couple returned during the day without making any discoveries as to our whereabouts. This was very alarming intelligence and, what increased their anxiety, there were seen floating on the Mersey blocks of wood and other substances which led some people to conjecture at once were the remains of the *Cavan*. In the meantime one vessel, the *Leitrim* sent to our assistance, had passed us in the fog and having gone a tolerably good distance on, without any hope of recovery, returned again. When suddenly they descried the brave *Cavan* battling against the waves, and for every one mile it went onward was drifted backward about five with the tide.

The *Cavan* was then joined to the *Leitrim* (by means of an immense cable) and as it towed us along to add to our comfort the rope gave way. At last by dint of great struggles and when almost every misadventure possible had occurred, about 4 p.m. we found ourselves sailing on gallantly towards our longed for destination. The next cause of distress was to discover the *Floridian* a little distance from us on route to New Orleans. Of course natural to suppose *our company's* first thought was what *would* become of us; when to our great relief the captain of the *Floridian* sent a message that he would await our arrival until 8 p.m. at a certain place down the Mersey. It now occurred to us it may be well to write our letters. Perhaps we would not have another opportunity. We accordingly took this chance to effect our purpose. Our forethought proved very successful, as having no sooner stepped on shore from the *Cavan* than we had to embark on a tug boat, *The Iron King*, which lay in readiness for us, having been prepared by one of the company's officials, who accompanied us down to the *Floridian* and saw that we were safely on board. Tea being over when we arrived, the stewardess prepared a special repast for us which consisted of some cold meats and tea.

After doing ample justice to it (You must remember we got nothing to eat or drink since morning and then had only a cup of tea) we retired to our cabins for the night and many a fervent D[eo]. G[ratias]. was uttered when we were landed safely in our berths. As after all the tossing about we *did* feel a *little* tired. Miss Fl[anagan], the two Marys, and Nora Q[uilter] are in one cabin. Nora P[rendiville] and I have one to ourselves. I now feel a little indisposed and having related all our nautical adventures up to the present I shall say goodnight. Our travels today amounted to 160 miles.

Friday 13

We arose this morning about 7.30, all excepting Miss Fl[anagan], feeling very nasty (a nautical expression). At 8 o'clock the first bell for breakfast rang, at 8.30 the second, at which having finished our toilet etc., we presented ourselves in the saloon not feeling much inclined to partake of the very enticing repast laid before us. Notwithstanding it was Friday, there were various meats laid for breakfast. There was also a variety of fish. The captain and officers, of course, took breakfast with the passengers who are only sixteen in number; none but first class being taken. They never have any steerage on this vessel. We had a view of the Wicklow mountains on our right and the Welsh on our left this morning when we went on deck. About midday we lost sight of all land. One of the passengers on board is a Frenchman. It may seem very rude of me, but I enjoy myself laughing at him when he tries to make himself understood. Especially at table he seems very hard up. I sit beside him and am often tempted to display some of my knowledge of his native language, but I fear 'a little learning is a dangerous thing'[6] would prove but too true in my case so that I have refrained from disgracing myself up to the present. Breakfast passed over very quietly. There was very little spoken; all seemed intent on their business. We were all beginning to feel very sick about luncheon time which is at 1 o'clock. However we tried to put in an appearance at table. After this we were completely knocked up and could not appear at either dinner or tea. All dine at 5 p.m. and take tea at 8 o'clock. We were very sick this evening, of course excepting Miss Fl[anagan], and retired pretty early. The extent of today's journey, that is counting from noon yesterday to the same time today, was 160 miles.

Saturday 14

None of us felt much better this morning and were unable to present ourselves even at breakfast; what would we not give to be able to stand steady for even a minute. I laughed at some of the others in the beginning but indeed I'll never again laugh at anybody that is seasick. It is simply dreadful. I was not present at luncheon either, but I believe the Irish and Home Rule were the topic. I have not heard in detail all that was said but have been told Mr Gladstone was completely cut.[7] Some at table who (I presume) were not interested in either side wished him dead twenty years ago. The initials given for him were G. O. M. These were interpreted by some part of the company as meaning good old man and by others as God's only mistake. There is an Englishman on board who got greatly excited over the matter so it was soon dropped. We all felt very ill all this day, appearing neither at dinner or tea, and in this critical condition thought it better to retire early. 282 miles today.

Sunday 15
What a contrast. Sunday morning in Cabra and Sunday morning on board the *Floridian* tossing about the broad Atlantic. We rose about 7 o'clock this morning and went on deck feeling very nasty but still something better. The morning was delightful, a cloudless sky and calm sea which up to the present has been unusually calm. I trust it will continue. We did not present ourselves at breakfast this morning but felt inclined for our other meals. All of which passed over very quietly. There seems always to be very little spoken. I was in a very talkative mood during this day, particularly at table; but I felt quite shy being the only person so disposed. It seemed to me I was entirely out of place. I don't mean anybody to infer from my anxiety to talk that I was not [as] disposed for enjoying myself as the rest of the company at table, but in my state of convalescence I thought I was quite capable of doing two things at a time. The evening passed very quietly with us. Nothing interesting happened. Not being quite convalescent we retired about 9 o'clock. 291 miles today.

Monday 16
A lovely morning on the Atlantic. The sea was perfectly smooth this morning. Just like a sheet of

glass; not a ripple on its surface, save where the vessel ploughing its way through the foaming brine caused it to divide on either side into high fleecy waves. The day slipped on very quietly, nothing strange coming with the wind. As the wind seems to be the only thing to cause a change on the ocean. Time hangs very heavily on our hands as we have no work. What possessed us to come without it? What would I not give for some knitting or sewing now. The only amusement we have is reading. Up to the present we were not inclined to indulge much in that owing to our seasickness. There is no library on board, but the captain and officers oblige us with books and papers. Otherwise we would feel the want of them very much. The company on board are very kind to us and very agreeable.

We understood in the beginning [that] our journey would last only fourteen days, but have been lately informed we will be on sea until the tenth of October. This is indeed a very unwelcome intelligence. We cleared 288 miles today.

Tuesday 17
The sea this morning was very glassy but when compared with yesterday it might be considered somewhat rough. The sky in the early morn was beautifully clear until about 8 o'clock, when the vessel became suddenly enveloped in a dense fog which continued for several hours. We have a Protestant minister with his wife and three children on board. The youngest child is a squalling infant in a perambulator. Rev T. R. Picot (the minister) is very kind but still does not exactly coincide with our tastes. He thought to catechise us on Saturday last

but evidently has had proof the mission would be a failure as he has not broached the subject since and I feel confident he won't do so either. We have a Scotch lady and gentleman travelling with us, the former on her way to Jamaica the latter to New Orleans. Nothing interesting has happened today. I fear the days will be very monotonous now for some time. In this day's journey, we cleared 287 miles.

Wednesday 18
This morning at 2 o'clock our vessel sighted the Azores at a distance of three miles west. A species of fish called porpoises are abundant in this part of the ocean. Some days, indeed, almost every day we sight some vessel or another either bound for or returning from America; it is very interesting to watch how they salute each other. All have a different way of saluting, some by the manner in which they hoist their flag, and others by the number of times it is hoisted. The time seems very long to us having nothing to do. Nora and I never tire asking all sorts of questions about the different parts of the ship and the particular uses of the various machines. The captain and officers are very kind and explain everything fully. By the time we will reach our journey's end, I think Nora and I will be able to steer a ship ourselves. I fear though it would be 'The Ship That Will Never Return.' We remained upon deck tonight until a very late hour viewing the stars. They are simply exquisite. It put me in mind so much of old times in Cabra when the dear old first class used to go out with poor S[ister] M[ary] Columba to view the different constellations. I could almost wish old times were back again. We travelled only 279 miles today; that is

counting from midday on yesterday to midday today, as that is the way they reckon every day's journey. You will notice we are not quite up to previous numbers. 'But shure the horse is doin' its best.'

Thursday 19
We went up on deck this morning at about 6.30 (Cabra time which I have kept and mean to keep until I reach N[ew] O[rleans]). The sun shone in all its splendour. The morning was beautifully fine, the sea quite placid, and the sky almost cloudless save touching the horizon [where] may be observed white fleecy clouds which give such an air of lightness to the scene. The heat during the day was oppressive, but I fear it was slightly so in comparison to what we will yet have to endure. The evenings up to the present are most delightful only they are so very short. All during the day, even when the heat is most intense, we have a little breeze but about five or half past five it becomes so cool and refreshing. I often wish we could bring the seniors out here for their night recreation. I can easily imagine how they would enjoy the scene (of course one of the nuns need not come). I would take it on myself to guard, and I'd send Nora to guard the juniors as I consider myself her senior during the voyage being appointed Mistress of Novices by Sr M Columba (McDonnel[l]) during our trip. We are getting to like sea life more and more every day since we got over our seasickness. We are enjoying our time immensely, but sometimes we are greatly perplexed as to 'How we shall get through the day.' I played a game of draughts tonight with Miss Fl[anagan]. Evidently from the excitment which our game caused, they are

very seldom played on board. 1 got game and felt very much sold at not having played for something. The next time I try them I shall be sure not to allow Miss Fl[anagan] to get off so easily.

Friday 20

A marvellous discovery. This morning after breakfast Nora found there was some material for making 'Agnus Deis' in her workbasket. This was of no small gratification to us as we would have something to do for a little time at least. It also occurred to us we could put our marks on the clothes that were in our cabin trunks. Perhaps when we have those things all finished some other very wonderful discovery might be effected. We have entered a part of the ocean now known as the Sargasso Sea. The surface of the water being in some places almost covered with a grasslike, weedy substance found principally in the Gulf of Mexico and floats about into the Atlantic. We've seen no other species of fish as yet, save the porpoises and a little tiny flying fish about the size of a butterfly. It has a white colour and jumps or flies about the surface of the water. This afternoon we had for the first time since we left home a very heavy shower of rain. Nora and I were leaning over the railing [a]round the deck admiring the beauties of the sky and sea and indulging in a little chat about old times (never to come again), when we noticed we were getting into a little mist or fog as we thought. One of the adjacent lifeboats partly covered us and, before we had time to consider, the rain fell in torrents. The part of the deck where we stood was like a little sea. It was only then it occurred to us we ought to seek for shelter in our cabin. So we ran for our lives and saw to our great mortification that the others had a good laugh at our expense. I assure you we won't be caught in a like net again. Nora and I had a long chat with the captain this evening. He told us of some of his nautical adventures and also the rates at which different vessels (our own included) travel and the dangers incurred by too speedy vessels. We also spoke of the political affairs of Ireland and England. (Just picture Nora and I doing two able politicians.) The captain's ideas of the treatment of the Irish we consider very fair in most points. He himself is a native of Devonshire but is so very genial looking and good natured; did we not know otherwise, we would feel certain he was an Irishman. He is a gentleman about fifty years of age, very kind and social. We all feel quite at home with him. N[ora] and I sometimes feel very shy asking him for an explanation of any new instrument used on board which we did not notice before. He seems to admire our ambition for knowledge and explains everything very clearly. The stars tonight were very numerous and quite distinct. It is a lovely night at sea; I trust you have as enjoyable a one on land.

Saturday 21

The appearance presented by the heavens this morning was most striking. The light but clear blue of the sky, intermingled with the snowy white soft clouds with which the sky was thinly studded, contrasted with the much deeper hue of the water beneath. Suddenly, in the dim west, we noticed it became quite cloudy immediately over the track which our gallant vessel was about to trace on the unrippled surface of the waters. Just then a magnificent rainbow was spanning the heavens to a great extent. However, as we expected, the rain did not fall right then but during the day. We had one or two rather heavy showers which did in no wise lessen the brightness of the scene, as they never continued longer than twelve or fifteen minutes and immediately on ceasing the sun burst forth in all its splendour and majesty. Indeed we would not regret if it did not shine so brilliantly, as the heat is becoming most intense especially we being almost always on deck. The cabins are very much confined; the portholes, being so small, can admit only a very limited amount of fresh air. The saloon too is rather close. We feel very much puzzled now-a-days for some news for our diaries. I fear they are most disinteresting especially these days [when] nothing, even the most trivial, has happened to break the monotony of the old routine. Our spirits are buoyed up with the hope of finding something interesting to tell you concerning the islands among which we expect to enter very soon.

Sunday 22

Our second Sunday tossing about on the bounding billow. Well, it did not seem so dreary and endless as last Sunday, but oh we do feel so very strange and lonely without hearing Mass. Why, it doesn't feel like Sunday at all. Nora and I commenced the day by taking baths. I had mine at 6.30. The water which we got was salt. We liked that, particularly not having expected it. We felt much refreshed after taking it. The weather is so intensely warm. The sea was a little rough this morning. Indeed the least ripple on its surface now we would consider rough being so much accustomed to a quite placid sea. A few showers of rain cooled the atmosphere at intervals during the day, and a beautiful atmosphere tinted the heavens. We read and played draughts for the greater part of the day. Nora and I were playing a game when Mr Picot (Junior), a chap about eight years of age, and his sister, a young lady who might be about five, came over and admonished us for playing—saying it was a sin to do so on Sunday. Their Papa told them so. Still they did not decline looking on at the game. We soon let them know if it were a sin to play it was equally as bad to look on. They then ran off and viewed us from a distance and seemed quite grieved [that] we should run headlong into destruction. They think we are much to be pitied in our religious blindness. The minister and his wife, also the Scotch lady and gentleman, did nothing but walk and talk. They would neither read or have any other amusement lest they should break the Sabbath. We enjoyed very much this afternoon, watching one of the officers trying with a grappling hook to arrest some of the Sargasso seaweed. Owing to the motion of our vessel as it sped along, he found it very difficult to obtain any. Indeed I think his endeavours were quite fruitless. We hope to be entertained with a like performance tomorrow. It was a cause of great amusement to watch such a proceeding, though I am sure you would think it a very foolish occupation. We remained on deck until a very late hour tonight. Our travels today 293 miles.

Wednesday 25
The last two days passed on much the same as usual. The morning about 7.30 we sighted a very small

island containing a lighthouse and what the inhabitants term a town, about six or eight houses. The island was very small and seemed to us to be made up of nothing but rocks, but I believe there are found on it mines out of which is dug a kind of phosphorous which is very valuable to the inhabitants. This island must be a Spanish possession as its name signifies the Spanish for hat.[8] We coasted several islands during the day, all inhabited and seemed to consist of prodigious rocks covered with a brown heath-like substance. They appeared to be very hilly. It was only on their shores [that] there appeared anything like what we would term grass. The sight of these islands had a very depressive effect on my spirits. They put me in mind so much of dear old Ireland, at the same time being so unlike it. There was such a vast difference between them and our green native shores. At about 3 p.m. we sighted St Thomas Island, our first calling port, and entered the harbour about a quarter past three. Our vessel cast anchor at about a distance of ten minutes rowing from the shore. We then saluted by firing two shots. The little town, known by the name of the island, presents a very nice appearance from sea. It is built at the base of a mountain. Indeed the island seems to be one unbroken chain of m[oun]t[ain]s, and on its slope the little town is situated. Shortly after we cast anchor about a dozen boats were rowed out by the blacks. This is customary when any vessel comes into port in case some of the passengers would wish to go ashore. Having such a good opportunity we thought to avail ourselves of it; and the Frenchman, Mr and Mrs Picot (the minister), Miss Fl[anagan]., Nora, and I went ashore. We were rowed in by one of the niggers. On coming near land the sea lost its beautiful blue colour and now appeared quite green. Viewed from our little boat, the town presented a magnificent appearance. It is almost crescent shaped. The houses are arranged in terraces like, one above the other and are built of wood, some white, blue, grey, and slate coloured etc., the roofs being nearly always red. The houses are all very low even with two stories; save in the shop windows, very few have glass in them. The others have a kind of shutter somewhat like Venetian blinds. These, of course, admit the air while they keep out the sun and rays. The streets are nearly all paved, where we have flags[tones]. Scarcely any of the houses have more than two storeys. The largest house I saw was an hotel; this had only two storeys. Also, if any person wants to take any refreshment such as soda water etc., he must take it outside the door. It looks so funny to see people sitting at tables out in the street taking their refreshments. We visited the Catholic church. It was nice enough for that place, but in Ireland we would be ashamed of it. There were three doors in front, the centre one largest. Over it is the organ gallery. At the sides are the windows; they have no glass in them or shutters either. I suppose at night they put up shutters. At one side there was a door opening into a flower garden. There were three altars, one of the side ones dedicated to the Blessed Virgin. This they were decorating for a feast which commenced on Friday and continued until Sunday. The back of the altar was all draped with pink and white muslin caught up with white and red paper roses. All paper flowers they had dressing the altar. They seem to have a great devotion to Our Lady of

Perpetual Succour.[9] There was a picture of her over the large altar. I also saw a banner with the like picture on it. I think they have only two priests as I saw only two confessionals. Most of the people are black; I met about six white people altogether. We looked so funny dressed in black and the sun scorching.

All the inhabitants there wear white. Even the men wear all white. The greater number wear no shoes, even ladies with hats on them. The poorer classes wear kerchiefs on their heads. The women go about with trays on their heads containing bread, cakes, sweets, and other commodities. We seemed quite a curiosity, even though people often call there when a ship goes into port. The inhabitants are quite friendly there and salute all the passersby. They speak nearly all French and Dutch, scarcely any English and that little badly. They are very obliging but great cheats if a stranger wished to buy anything from them, although it's a free port. They pay no duty on goods. All the women and a number of the men wear earrings, even the little babies only a few days old. They have some superstition about it. Some are real jet black. All have woolly hair but exquisite eyes and teeth. Oh such exquisite eyes. We returned to our ship about quarter past five. We had only about an hour and a half to see the town. The captain meant to start at 5 p.m. but having to unload a large amount of cargo is not prepared to start until tomorrow morning about 5. From where we lay at anchor the view of the town, when lighted up at night, is magnificent. The dark lofty mountains in the background, then the rows of houses one above another was [sic] just like an altar when the several rows of candles are burning on it. Then the cloudless sky, all studded with stars. The night is beautifully calm and the water quite still. The bells of the Catholic church and Protestant chapel chime every hour. Tonight we stayed on deck until midnight admiring the beautiful scene. This even[ing] we got seventeen passengers on board. They are all blacks who had been staying in St Thomas for some time. I had no opportunity of taking a good view of them this evening so that I shall furnish a glowing account of them in tomorrow's diary.

Thursday 26
This morning, at a very early hour, I was awakened from my refreshing slumbers by a kind of noise that I really did not know what it was. I listened attentively and soon discovered it to be a number of persons crying, so I thought; but it, I believe, was meant to be singing. A number of children owned by some blacks who came on board yesterday gave the entertainment which commenced in the early part of the night and continued until morning. Those whose berths were near, I fear, suffered much; wherein we who were so far away were roused at such an unseasonable hour. We have three men on board. Two are real tawnies. The other is jet black; he is a doctor and quite a young fellow. The elder of the two others is a minister and has a wife and family on board. There are I think four married women (including the minister's wife) amongst them and two or three girls. The remainder are children. They are most peculiar beings (I don't care to use the word despicable though it is the more appropriate) I ever

beheld both in manners and appearance. Their manners amongst themselves are very coarse and indelicate, no kind of decency being observed particularly amongst the children. They are very slovenly and lazy. They throw themselves about the deck in all possible attitudes and positions. They are very social towards us, if we encouraged them, but indeed we keep from them as much as possible. None of the company on board can tolerate them. It is amusing to see all the white people keeping to themselves in one part of the deck and all the blacks in another. They seem to be people of a very wealth[y] class to judge from the amount of jewellery the[y] wear and the style in which they dress. If the manners of people in their position be such as we have witnessed, what kind must the low classes be. They have been in St Thomas for some time it appears. When there is any disturbance in any of those islands the inhabitants, who can afford and whose position will allow it, leave the island until the place becomes quietened; then they return. The election of a president was the cause of our present company's leaving. The weather is becoming warmer every hour, I think; the heat is terrific. Just imagine, we are now getting in amongst the West Indies. We will be parting with some of our passengers at the different ports where we will call. Only the six of us and another gentleman will be going to New Orleans unless we take up any passengers at the ports. Nora has go[t] neuralgia for the past week. On that account we retire[d] early those nights.

Friday 27
My previous attempt to describe the heavens in the

morning at or after sunrise were I think a complete failure. At all events they were in no way up to the mark or as I would wish them to be. So after so many repeated failures I shall not again attempt the like project, but will leave you to imagine its beauty as I cannot find words to describe it. It seems to me to be growing nicer everyday. I think I would not mind now if I had to live my whole life on sea, if that could possibly be managed. The sunrise and sunsets are so magnificent. Oh, but the heat is terrific. We are actually melting. This morning when we went on deck we had a view of San Domingo. We were quite near the coast and will be so for two or three days, as we are to sail nearly all [a]round it having to call at different ports the first of which we will arrive at tomorrow morning. It is know[n] as Gonaïves where we expect to delay for two or three days to unload some cargo, consisting of four immense cargo boats and about forty tons of coal, that will take some time to put out. This day passed on much the same as usual, save that we had a little diversion watching the blacks. I can't endure them, notwithstanding all the fun they create. This afternoon as Nora and I went on deck after luncheon, feeling quite out of sorts having nothing to read as we finished with the stack of books we had. The captain kindly called us into his little sitting room on deck. (You know it is quite a privilege to get in there.) He opened a press which was plentifully stored with a nice selection of books and asked us to take whatever ones we wished for and whatever number we wanted. Indeed that was a godsend at such a time. We did not fail to express our warmest thanks to the captain. We also felt very much honoured with our privilege. Tonight, at about 6 p.m. we noticed a kind of lightning in the direction of San Domingo which lay to our left. It did not pass in flashes b[ut] seemed to illumine the heavens to a great extent at intervals, for about a second, and then would disappear. We watched it until about 10 o'clock with great interest. It is the first we have had since we set out. The sea was quite smooth and without any indications of a storm. I think it will continue so during the night. However, even if the weather do[es] change, we are quite at our ease. We feel as if nothing could happen to us. It may prove unluck[y] to be over confident.

Saturday 28
Notwithstanding we half expected it, we did not have a storm last night. It was rather a pleasant night at sea. Early this morning, as we anticipated, our vessel arrived at Gonaïves. After all necessary preparations were gone through, we cast anchor at about a quarter of an hour rowing from the little town; then the minute gun was fired for the royal salute. We had a good view of the town. It is very small and dirty. We were advised not to go ashore; it was such a miserable place and there was nothing worth seeing. There were several vessels in the harbour with ours; one was an American man-of-war. We took particular stock of it, never having seen one before. The others were almost all European vessels. We spent nearly the whole day watching them; it was nice to note their different flags etc. There were little boats coming from and returning to the shore all during the day. It occupied the whole day, from the time anchor was cast until about 6 o'clock this evening, to unload three boats. That will,

I am sure, give you an idea of their immense size. Tomorrow the fourth boat and the coal will be unloaded. Sunday and Monday are all the same on board. One or two blacks went away this morning, a lady and gentleman—brother and sister—both coming from Paris; but we got two ladies and six gentlemen to make up for them. There are more expected tomorrow. Tonight too we had terrific lightning, but I believe it was not dangerous. We did not care to remain on deck long tonight on account of the lightning, though otherwise it is a glorious night.

Sunday 29

Sunday morning, our third on board the *Floridian*. Since we've got accustomed to it, it's not so bad. Oh, but we do feel so much not having Mass. Next Sunday will be our last. We are sorry in some ways and in others delighted. This is Michaelmas day too.[10] Early this morning we were wakened with the noise, as they were heaving out the coal etc. This process continued until 1 p.m. It was not very pleasant to be on deck then, as the dust of the coal was blowing about in all directions. But, in the evening, it was rather nice. We had a good view of the town, which was not much to be seen, but the surrounding country was exquisite. It seemed very fertile in the lowlands which surrounded the town. The whole country seems very hilly [a]round the coasts. But from some people on board, who know the place very well, I have heard it is a beautiful country, very productive and also well cultivated. Surprising[ly] the coasts are so densely surrounded with hills. It renders the towns on the coast very unhealthy. At about 6.30 we set sail. It was an exquisite evening. Everything seemed so still. We had a fair share of lightning; the moon and stars too were exquisite. It was a heavenly night. We often wish we could bring Cabra and its inmates out here for a night. Indeed I know how all would enjoy the scene.

Monday 30

Early this morning we landed in Port-au-Prince. It is a nice little town when viewed from the sea at a little distance; but to dwell in, I believe, is not so pleasant. We could not go ashore to our regret. On making some inquiries about it Mr Picot (the minister), who is a native of the place, informed us it is a nice place to live in. But I believe his idea of it is that it ranks next to Paris. This is really his idea, but the captain told us it is a miserable place. The streets are not even paved but are all covered with sand. The houses are pretty nice. There is a cathedral built in the old French style and two Catholic churches.[11] The country [a]round P[ort]-a[u]-P[rince], like the surroundings of the other ports, seems very hilly; but over these hills the country is simply delightful and tolerably cool in parts. We've seen and eaten too a great variety of fruits obtained at the different ports. We got some very delightful bananas. They grow wild in these islands. We saw some green oranges just as they were taken from the trees, with the leaves hanging on to them. We also got some pineapples, a peculiar kind of pear with a nut inside,[12] shaddock and several other kinds of which we don't know the names.

Mr Picot and family left this morning, also some couple of negro families who came from Gonaïves. But indeed I regret to say we won't be lonely after them, as about seventy others came on board this evening. Of course there are not sufficient cabins in the vessel for that number, but some came for deck passengers. That is, they are boarded in the vessel like the other passengers but sleep on deck. The company make[s] any amount of money in this way. But such a variety as we have got on board today, old and young, tall and small, fat and lean, and such a variety of styles and colours and shapes and forms and figures. I won't venture to describe them. If I did, I don't know when I should be finished; it would be a long time before I would, I fear. As for luggage Mrs Browne's wouldn't hold [a] candlelight for any single one of them.[13] We are sick laughing at them. We set sail again this evening about 5 p.m. and expect to arrive at the next port tomorrow morning.

Tuesday 1 Oct

At about 6 a.m. this morning we arrived at our third [and] last [Haitian] port, before New Orleans, known by the name of Jérémie. It is rather a small unimport[ant] place. All these ports seem to be built along the coasts. They are much longer than wide. We had a delay here of about four or five hours; there were about forty tons of cargo to put out. These ports are so disturbed on account of the revolution. It would be most dangerous to go ashore; therefore, we had to deny ourselves that pleasure. From where we lay an anchor it did not present a very nice appearance; and I believe on entering it, it presents a much less pleasing appearance. Only one or two officers and some sailors went ashore. The day passed as usual, nothing strange happening. We set sail about 3 p.m. We spend the greater part of our time watching the blacks on the lower decks, where some who cannot pay for first class have to remain. The decks serve for dormitories, saloons and everything else they want. I do believe they are half savages. A shark came about the vessel while it lay at anchor. It was the first we have ever seen. It was only a young one; it might measure about six feet in length. The evenings are getting very short now. The nights are delightful and holding up very fine.

Wednesday 2

We arrived at about 6.30 in Jacmel. This is a rather small port and has a most dangerous harbour. The houses are much higher than those in any of the ports we have passed yet, but in any other respect I think it did not differ. We had a delay of about three or four hours while the cargo was being unloaded. At about 3 o'clock we again set sail. This day too passed very quietly. Of course calling to the different ports is a great variety; but still when we don't go ashore there is not much to be seen, save the outskirts of the towns themselves and the surrounding country which looks much fresher and seems better cultivated than the other parts of Haiti. This evening was beautiful. It was very pleasant on deck in the evening, about 6 o'clock, as it was then very cool. The blacks were very industrious, making active preparations for their landing at home tomorrow. It was most amusing to watch them. They quietened down very early, though I daresay they liked to look a little fresh in the morning. Those on deck got no slight touch of a shower bath during the night, at about 2 a.m. There were two pretty heavy showers, but they did not continue long. Showers are sometimes most welcome in this part of the country; in excessive heat, they are most refreshing. The blacks seem never afraid of catching cold. We have not forgotten [that] our old companions in the Immaculata have entered into their retreat this evening. Our thoughts are with them tonight. I trust they will remember old friends in their prayers.

Thursday 3

This morning, when we rose about 6 o'clock, we had quite a near view of the coast of Jamaica. At about 8 a.m. we sighted Kingston and Port Royal from that distance. The former seemed quite near and the latter a good distance off. While on the contrary, the port was nearer us than the capital. Port Royal is built on a very narrow portion of the coast, jutting far out into the sea. It was much more important some time ago than it is at present. However it represents a very nice appearance now. We arrived there at about 10 o'clock, not touching near the coast having no cargo to unload there. But all vessels entering Kingston must anchor there for some time. We anchored for about quarter of an hour. A doctor came on board who had to see all the passengers for Kingston, which constituted all the blacks, the Scotch lady, and the Englishman who came from Liverpool with us. A ferry boat travels from Kingston to Port Royal several times during the day; numbers of people go out there on pleasure trips. At about 11 o'clock we anchored at Kingston, where all passengers on board left save our six and the Scotchman. We are such a little company now. It took a long time to put out the luggage. It was very amusing to watch the *unloading* of the blacks and their cargo. The luggage in some cases being much more presentable than the owners. When all this was over, which was not until about 1 o'clock, the crew began to unload the cargo. We are quite close to the town. The companies who own our vessel have a dock there so that we can step ashore any time we wish while in the harbour.

After luncheon all the six of us went out to see the town. We took a drive in one of the tram cars through the principal part of the town. We also visited the garden which I shall describe fully tomorrow. We visited the Catholic church which is a very nice building, also the convent of the Sisters of the Immaculate Conception. We were present in their little church for Benediction at 4 o'clock. Just imagine the treat that was to us, after our three weeks on sea without Mass or Benediction. The town seems to be a very businesslike place during the day. People don't seem to mind the heat much. It was lovely tonight in the harbour; everything was so quiet and still. It was a beautiful moonlight night too. A moonlight night at sea is something exquisite indeed. Every night we've had on sea was almost indescribable. The captain has remarked several times what a grand voyage we were getting. We had the presumption to say it was because we were on board. I feel very tired and sleepy after the walk today, and it was so excessively warm so I shall say goodnight.

Friday 4

Last night Nora and I had been planning for having what we would call a *good day*. So we rose this morning in excellent health and spirits, D[eo]. G[ratias]., with delight at the prospect of such an expedition as we intended to go on. We set out immediately after breakfast and visited the principal streets, notwithstanding it was so excessively warm. We walked through almost all the town. The streets are very rough and dirty; no such thing as tiles or flags[tones] of any description to be seen. The town is very large, but the streets are very disunited in some places [with] a part of a road intervening them. The houses are very low and almost all built of wood. There are some few built of bricks, [and] the greater number are roofed with galvanized iron. The public gardens, though small, are very cool and nicely kept. Every part of them [are] shaded with trees of which there are a great variety: the breadfruit, date palm, African oil palm, cocoanut, casuarine, long bean, and bananas. There are also several other kinds of which we don't know the names. There are a great variety of flowers and other plants. In it also [are] a couple of fountains. The cactus plant grows wild here and is used for fencing or hedging. Of course some of it is cultivated in the gardens too, but people think nothing of it here. After resting and refreshing ourselves in the garden, we set out again to see some of the town we had not already visited. We went to the church and, just imagine, there was Exposition of the Most Blessed Sacrament; I suppose it's being the first Friday of the month. Aren't we fortunate beings after all. Having spent this much time in sightseeing through the town, we now thought perhaps we could find something worth seeing in the country. We therefore hired a bus.[14] This is sort of a vehicle covered overhead and at the back, with little curtains at the side which draw the wind; only about two or three can sit in them. I am sure I need not say how Nora and I enjoyed our drive. We had the best of fun.

it should be very bad indeed when we would not enjoy it.

During the drive we saw several very nice places. We passed by the black soldiers' camp[15] and the race course and saw an endless variety of plants and shrubs. We did not return home until about 5 o'clock, just in time for dinner. Indeed we made the *most* of everything. Oh, how we did enjoy it. We could see where the English soldiers' camp was situated from the vessel. It is up on the side of a mountain about 4000 feet high. They have been sent up there for their health and to keep them out of the reach of getting sickness. Notwithstanding all our going about, we stayed on deck tonight until 11 o'clock. The moon and stars are exquisite. How I wish you could witness the scene. It is something superb. You would never tire looking at it. Necessity compelled us to leave it even at the late hour we did.

Saturday 5

The unloading of the cargo for Kingston not being finished, we were obliged to remain longer than we expected in consequence. After the cargo was all unloaded, the ship was again reloaded with oranges for New Orleans to the amount of about a thousand casks. In consequence of this we could not resume our journey onward until Saturday afternoon.

Wednesday 9

This morning about daybreak our vessel sailed into the Mississippi. New Orleans is situated about ninety-five miles up the river. After going a distance of some miles up its course, a doctor come on board who had to see all the passengers and crew. This was

about 6 o'clock. We sailed on then to about twenty
miles up the river when another doctor came on
board who had to see us also. Here then the vessel
had to anchor beside a dock for 'quarantine,' as it's
called. This is a process every vessel going into New
Orleans has to go through. It consists in this. Every
passenger and every member of the crew have to
take out all their clothing—worn or not, new or old—
and hang them on racks prepared for the purpose.
These racks are fixed at the mouths of immense
cylinders constructed of metal pipes about two
inches in diameter. These pipes are covered on the
outside with a thick kind of canvas.

Through these pipes are passed the fumes of
sulphur and other purifying substances. These fumes
hav[e] a temperature of about 120 [degrees]. The
racks are so prepared that they can be drawn in and
out of these cylinders. Each person places his or her
clothes on a rack; the racks are then drawn into the
cylinders, which are closed air tight. The fumes are
sent through the pipes for about three quarters of an
hour. The racks are then drawn out, and the clothes
allowed to air for a few minutes. Of course they are
burning hot when they are drawn out. Each person
has then to change the clothes he has on. These are
now sent in to be fumigated.

Not alone our clothes, which are made and which
we have been wearing, but every piece in the shape
of clothing. Our trunks, which were down in the
hold, had to be taken out and everything in them
unpacked and fumigated. I need not say they were
not improved by the process. Some of the finer
material was very much crushed, but there is no
option in the matter. It must be gone through; it is the

custom of the country. There is no means of getting out of it either, as everything in the shape of beds, cloth goods, etc. have [sic] to be taken out and fumigated. While this is being done, there are tubes containing sulphurous water passed in through every part of the vessel—saloons, cabins, etc.—which are all sprinkled with it. There are also immense metal pipes passed into the holds and lower parts of the ship, and sulphur fumes [are] sent through.

When all this process is gone through, the vessel sails from the dock out into the river to a small distance where it has to remain stationary for five days to get quite free from any infection it may have taken in during the voyage. This fumigating business commences in May and continues until 1 November. This is the third voyage with the *Floridian* and the third time with it being fumigated. For every time a vessel is fumigated the company that owns it have [sic] to pay 160 dollars. So you can easily imagine how the state makes money in that way. Three or four vessels come in some days. All the money goes to the state.

We expect to get away on Sunday morning. And now having reached our journey's end I trust you will be pleased with my endeavours to relate as best I could our adventures during the voyage. I have done my very best to make it interesting. Please don't criticise [it] *too severely*. May I hope my endeavours will not prove an utter failure.

Notes

1 The image of Eve has been one of weakness and fallibility.
2 The dock-street on the north bank of the River Liffey, in

the port of Dublin, from which many Irish emigrants began their voyage to America.

3 The expectation was that they would never return to Ireland. The fact that Nora did (once) was unusual. Most women who entered religious communities, especially cloistered ones, in the nineteenth and early twentieth centuries did not return.

4 These lines are written in a script that is different from the remainder of the text—probably copied from a book read on the *Floridian*.

5 Morpheus is the god of dreams in Ovid's *Metamorphoses*.

6 Taken from *An Essay on Criticism* by Alexander Pope (1688–1744). There was a strong French influence in convent boarding schools in Ireland during the late nineteenth century. The Dominican Sisters at Cabra, in particular, placed great emphasis on French culture. See especially Anne V. O'Connor, 'The Revolution in Girls' Secondary Education in Ireland, 1860–1910,' in Mary Cullen, ed., *Girls Don't Do Honours: Irish Women in Education in the 19th and 20th Centuries* (Dublin: Argus Press and Women's Education Bureau 1987), 39.

7 William E. Gladstone (1809–98) served as England's Liberal prime minister four times (1868–74, 1880–5, 1886, and 1892–94). His chief Irish opponent was nationalist Charles Stewart Parnell (1846–91) who served as member of the British parliament from 1875–91 and led Ireland's Home Rule movement.

8 Sombrero Island. See Nora's diary for 25 September.

9 It was not unusual for sailors and their families to have a special devotion to Our Lady of Perpetual Succour.

10 A feast observed in honour of the archangel Michael.

11 Besides the cathedral in the centre of Port-au-Prince, there were two other parishes—St Anne's in the southern section and St Joseph's in the northern. Pan American Union, *Haiti*, 34.

12 Most likely an avocado.

13 We are not certain of the identity of 'Mrs Browne.' In his collection of English diaries, Arthur Ponsonby describes a 'very entertaining little diary' kept by a Mrs Browne who accompaned Braddock's expedition to Virginia on board the London from 17 November 1754 to 4 August 1757. Perhaps Alice, Nora, and their Cabra friends had read a printed copy of this diary? See Arthur Ponsonby, ed., *English Diaries: A Review of English Diaries from the Sixteenth to the Twentieth Century* (London: Methuen and Company 1922), 220–24.

14 Omnibuses (or cabs) as well as hackney carriages could be hired for sightseeing tours. Ford and Cundall, *The Handbook of Jamaica*, 573–74.

15 At the end of the eighteenth century, natives were admitted to the West Indian Local Defence Forces but they had their own camps. Ford and Cundall, *The Handbook of Jamaica*, 579-80.

PART III

THE CHALLENGE OF RESEARCHING NUNS' LIVES

Margaret MacCurtain

When Nora and Alice sent back their diaries to Cabra, their accounts of weeks on board the *Floridian* reflected intelligent minds of young Irishwomen poised on the threshold of adult life in the final decade of the nineteenth century. Their diaries were not intimate memoirs in any literary sense; and perhaps because they appeared innocuous, so much in appearance—two black-covered copybooks—an extension of the school museum, they remained undisturbed among the convent records for over a century. Those who read them were most likely entertained by the artlessness and enthusiasm of the young authors, and then quietly returned the copybooks to their modest resting place. In actuality, the diaries provide a unique insight into the attitudes and intellectual curiosity of two young Irishwomen who belonged to a generation that entered the new century. Their schooling educated them to express themselves; to voice their opinions on a number of topics, including national politics and religion; and to articulate unselfconsciously their attitudes towards race and ethnicity even as they chose to settle in a region painfully marked by racial segregation.

Increasingly historians are examining diaries as valuable evidence from the past. With the publication of diaries, readers begin to appreciate the historical background that frames the thoughts expressed by the diarists. None escapes the culture of her times, and a diary affords the opportunity of looking through a contemporary window at a forgotten world. The greatest good fortune that befell Nora and Alice's diaries was their survival in the archives of a convent for over a hundred years.

All convents are obliged by ecclesiastical law to appoint an annalist. Either she, or another, is given the task of collecting and storing the documents and records relevant to the history of the major events that occur in the life of that community. Narrative in form, they become the basis for published histories.

All convent records are kept in a cupboard or room known simply as 'the archives.' Here are located the profession registers of the nuns, the account books, correspondence with ecclesiastical authorities and less official letters, and administrative material that deals with the leadership and the organisation of the religious order of which the convent is an organism. Despite the hazards of casual destruction, many convent archives contain photographs from the last century, school registers of nineteenth-century foundations, newspaper cuttings, old liturgical books, and even patterns of nuns' clothing long out of date.

In some convent traditions a nun's obituary, written by a well-informed member of the order, is kept in the archives. Occasionally, if a nun is prominent in educational or civic affairs, a newspaper will carry an account of her major activities and responsibilities. Thus Nora, Sister Patricia Prendiville, was accorded a lengthy appreciation in New Orleans' *Daily Picayune,* 21 May 1907, because she was headmistress of St Mary's Academy when she died. The death of Alice, Sister Columba Nolan, was noted in the same newspaper, 19 December 1910. The diaries of Nora and Alice, as already mentioned, along with school account books, old class photographs, and other nineteeth-century school memorabilia, are preserved in the Cabra convent archives. Lodged in the St Mary's archives in New Orleans is Nora's sketchbook of drawings (done while a boarder at Cabra), a period piece of more than passing curiosity.

One of the most significant developments in recent years has been the changed attitude of religious orders towards the preservation of their archives. David Sheehy, archivist of the Dublin Diocesan Archives and chair of the Irish Region of the Society of Archivists, attributes this enlightened outlook to a determined group of religious archivists who formed in 1979 the Association of Religious Archives of Ireland. Their purpose is to raise awareness among religious orders about the value of preserving and cataloguing their records. In 1985 the Association issued a draft 'Directory of Irish Religious Archives,' which partially revealed the substantial body of information that exists in convent archives. In 1992, in response to a wider understanding of the transdenominational nature of religious archives, the group became the Association of Church Archivists of Ireland. Practically it means that researchers no longer need to justify convent archives in terms of authenticity.

By the end of the nineteenth century convent life was attracting considerable numbers of young women to join religious orders and to take the three vows necessary for profession: poverty, chastity, and obedience. Though the life was arduous and placed much emphasis on asceticism, in particular fasting and relinquishing ownership of possessions, religious vocations continued to rise until well after the middle of the twentieth century. The statistics tell their own story. According to the 1901 Census there were 8,031 nuns in Ireland, an eightfold increase over the 1841 Census figures (987 nuns), despite an almost 50 per cent reduction in the Catholic population. In 1901 Ireland had 368 convents, the majority built along the architectural lines that Nora and Alice admired in Castleisland and Cabra. At the turn of the century there were 40,000 nuns in the United States; by 1915 the numbers had risen to 75,000.

Compared with Irish convent living, the flexibility of religious life for women in America was reflected, for instance, in the lighter apparel worn in New Orleans. But nearly everywhere in the New World there was less insistence on dowries for admission and less rigid codes of travelling and enclosure. Nuns were not only allowed but encouraged to go outside the convent precincts to work in parishes teeming with immigrants from Europe. The Vatican finally recognised 'active orders' of women as a canonical group distinct from the medieval contemplative orders of nuns who lived secluded within the cloister in 1900. According to the New Orleans convent annals, in 1910 the St Mary's Dominican nuns voted to abolish any difference in dress between choir and lay Sisters. Among those who supported this move were Alice (shortly before her sudden death) and Nora's two sisters, Sisters Gertrude and Teresa Prendiville. Active religious life devoted to teaching, hospital ministry, and work in custodial institutions remained for the greater part of the twentieth century a salient feature of Catholicism worldwide, attracting thousands of committed young women to enter the variety of religious communities that perceived themselves as 'active' in their mission.

How does the historian account for the rise in female vocations in a century that offered women more educational opportunities and a wider choice of work than ever before? Why were Irishwomen eager to leave Ireland to enter convents in the United States or elsewhere and, after World War I, to immerse themselves in the missionary projects of Africa, India, and the Far East? Did the creation of the Irish Free State after 1923 alter the emigrant or missionary experience? In *The Irish Missionary Movement* (Dublin, 1990), Edmund M. Hogan suggests that the high impulse of sacrificial duty, evident in the leaders of the 1916 Irish Rebellion, carried over to the generation that established the Irish Free State and found its fullest expression in the spread of missionary religious vocations in the subsequent decades. What insight into the Irish family is derived from the discovery that siblings often followed older sisters, aunts, or cousins to particular religious communities? These and other questions can and should be answered, and convent archives supply many clues.

Sometimes it can be misleading if the wrong question is put to material or if the techniques and skills of interpreting documents are inaccurately applied. Investigations of the past are most successful when new questions are asked about a familiar or, for that matter, hidden past. A fresh approach to recording the experience of Catholic nuns is contingent on a number of factors. There is, first and foremost, the availability of reliable sources. From the context in which the diaries of Nora and Alice were set, it is apparent that evidence from quite varied deposits was available.

Why is there an interest at this time in convent culture? There is, as David Sheehy remarked, a history industry since the 1960s that has given archives a new focus and has greatly widened the demand for access. There is also a return to and a development of the history of religion in its many forms. The present and next generation of researchers is looking for wider sources, such as convent and monastic archives, and new methods in an attempt to respond to fresh questions. Studies analysing religious belief and behaviour are made possible by the refinement of analytical and theoretical means of assessing quantitative material. This has opened up avenues hitherto unexplored.

In the history of emigration, prospective nuns—like Nora and Alice—were subsets of groups of women emigrating from Europe. Suellen Hoy, in her article on the emigration of nineteenth-century Irish religious women (*Journal of Women's History*, forthcoming), estimates that about 10 per cent of all nuns working in the United States in 1900 were Irish women who had emigrated as nuns, novices, postulants, or aspirants. The rise of feminist history and the parallel study of gender history in the 1980s has also influenced historical method. A feminist methodology studies the group, the life-cycle, the recurrent. For example, Caitriona Clear in *Nuns in Nineteenth-Century Ireland* (Dublin 1987) took a sample of nine convents and looked at nuns as women in their social and economic setting. Her examination of the dowry along with the difference between the work of choir and lay Sisters in turn begs further investigation into the construction of class in nineteenth-century Ireland.

Among the characteristics of the new approach to writing about nuns in the Catholic Church is the study of work-patterns in convent lifestyles as they evolved along professional lines from the beginning of the twentieth century. Nora and Alice had little difficulty in adjusting to the teaching requirements of New Orleans, not because these were particularly easy to acquire but rather because Irishwomen were English-speaking and well-educated before they emigrated. Both features, in fact, made them much sought after by religious recruiters during both the nineteenth and twentieth centuries.

The importance of unordained ministry for the twentieth-century Catholic Church is becoming recognized even as the parochial school or the convent boarding school disappears. There is an impression that religious life for women in twentieth-century Ireland was sterile and narcissistic and that women precipitated themselves into convents for family and economic reasons. The flow of vocations between 1870 and 1970, when a sharp decline was first observed, requires a different kind of analysis; and the research on which to base a viable interpretation has only begun.

In this quest we need to hear the voices of women who are nuns, especially the self who is no longer annalist but the subject of the testimony. The journals of nuns exist, as Nora and Alice's diaries lived on. We need to hear the voices of nuns released into familiar speech with their families and friends. There are letters in family collections that nuns have written, which record private feelings and thoughts; and there are others, which provide glimpses of spirituality, nuances of alternative realities for desolate hearts. With the growth of archival interest the preservation of informal records, such as emigrants' letters, oral interviews, old photographs, unpublished memoirs, make convent archives valuable resources for historians of religion, women, and emigration. The storing of such deposits and the training of those who look after them are further steps in extending awareness about the importance of keeping women's 'papers.'

Nora and Alice's diaries captivated us and then invited us to set them into context and to discover the underlying narrative of the writers' lives. Suellen Hoy's ability to prise out nuggets of information from seemingly impenetrable recesses has been one of the great pleasures of this collaborative work. A discovery by her or by the archivists of the two main deposits, Sister Terence O'Keeffe in Cabra and Sister Dorothy Dawes in New Orleans, challenged me to think again and anew about the lives of these two ordinary—or perhaps extraordinary—Irishwomen. Having tracked down every possible clue and combined all our insights, the story of Nora and Alice is ours to share with you.

SELECT BIBLIOGRAPHY

Clear, Catriona, *Nuns in Nineteenth-Century Ireland* (Dublin, 1987).

_____, 'The Limits of Female Autonomy: Nuns in Nineteenth-Century Ireland' in Maria Luddy and Cliona Murphy, eds., *Women Surviving: Studies in Irish Women's History in the 19th and 20th Centuries* (Dublin, 1989).

_____, 'Walls within Walls: Nuns in Nineteenth-Century Ireland,' in Chris Curtin, Pauline Jackson, and Barbara O'Connor, eds., *Gender in Irish Society* (Galway, 1987).

Corish, Patrick J, *The Irish Catholic Experience: A Historical Survey* (Wilmington, Delaware, 1985).

Diner, Hasia, *Erin's Daughters in America: Irish Immigrant Women in the Nineteenth Century* (Baltimore, 1983).

Dolan, Jay P., *The American Catholic Experience: A History from Colonial Times to the Present* (New York, 1985).

Eager, Irene Ffrench, *Margaret Anna Cusack: One Woman's Campaign for Women's Rights* (Dublin, 1979).

Fahey, Tony, 'Nuns in the Catholic Church in Ireland in the Nineteenth Century,' in Mary Cullen, ed., *Girls Don't Do Honours: Irish Women in Education in the 19th and 20th Centuries* (Dublin, 1987).

Fitzpatrick, David, '"A Share of the Honeycomb":

Education, Emigration and Irishwomen,' *Continuity and Change*, I, No. 2 (1986).

_____, 'Marriage in Post-famine Ireland,' in Art Cosgrove, ed., *Marriage in Ireland* (Dublin, 1985).

_____, 'The Modernisation of the Irish Female,' in *Rural Ireland, 1600–1900: Modernisation and Change* (Cork, 1987).

Hogan, Edmund M., *The Irish Missionary Movement: A Historical Survey, 1830–1980* (Dublin, 1990).

Hoy, Suellen, 'The Journey Out: The Recruitment and Emigration of Irish Religious Women to the United States, 1812–1914,' *Journal of Women's History* (forthcoming).

Jackson, Pauline, 'Women in the 19th Century Irish Emigration,' *International Migration Review*, XVIII (Winter, 1984).

Keenan, Desmond J., *The Catholic Church in Nineteenth-Century Ireland: A Sociological Study* (Totowa, New Jersey, 1983).

Larkin, Emmet, 'Church, State, and Nation in Modern Ireland,' in *The Historical Dimensions of Irish Catholicism* (Washington, D.C., 1976 and 1984).

_____, 'The Devotional Revolution in Ireland, 1850–75,' *American Historical Review*, 77 (June 1972).

Lavin, Mary, 'The Nun's Mother,' in *The Stories of Mary Lavin*, Volume 2 (London, 1974).

Lee, J. J., 'Women and the Church since the Famine,' in Margaret Mac Curtain and Donncha O'Corrain, eds., *Women in Irish Society: The Historical Dimension* (Westport, Connecticut, 1979).

Mageean, Deirdre, 'Catholic Sisterhoods and the

Immigrant Church,' in Donna Gabaccia, ed., *Seeking Common Ground: Multidisciplinary Studies of Immigrant Women in the United States* (Westport, Connecticut, 1992).

Miller, Kerby A., *Emigrants and Exiles: Ireland and the Irish Exodus to North America* (New York, 1985).

Nolan, Janet A., *Ourselves Alone: Women's Emigration from Ireland, 1885–1920* (Lexington, Kentucky, 1989).

Nugent, Walter, *Crossings: The Great Transatlantic Migrations, 1870–1914* (Bloomington, Indiana, 1992).

O'Brien, Kate, *The Land of Spices* (London, 1941 and 1991).

O'Brien, Susan, 'Terra Incognita: The Nun in Nineteenth-Century England,' *Past and Present*, 121 (Nov. 1988).

O'Carroll, Ide, *Models for Movers: Irish Women's Emigration to America* (Dublin, 1990).

O'Connor, Anne V., 'The Revolution in Girls' Secondary Education in Ireland, 1860–1910,' in Mary Cullen, ed., *Girls Don't Do Honours: Irish Women in Education in the 19th and 20th Centuries* (Dublin, 1987).

O'Flaherty, Liam, 'Going into Exile,' in Seamus Deane *et al.*, eds., *The Field Day Anthology of Irish Writing*, Vol. III (Derry, 1992).

Thompson, Margaret Susan, 'Cultural Conundrum: Sisters, Ethnicity, and the Adaptation of American Catholicism,' *Mid-America*, 74 (Oct. 1992).

_____, 'Philemon's Dilemma: Nuns and the Black Community in Nineteenth-Century America: Some Findings,' *Records of the American Catholic Historical Society of Philadelphia*, 96 (1986).

_____, 'Women, Feminism, and the New Religious History: Catholic Sisters as a Case Study,' in Philip R. Vandermeer and Robert P. Swierenga, *Belief and Behavior: Essays in the New Religious History* (New Brunswick, New Jersey, 1991).

White, Antonia, *Frost in May* (London, 1933 and 1991).

EMERGING FROM THE SHADOW

The lives of
Sarah Anne Lawrenson and Lucy Olive Kingston

Based on Personal Diaries, 1883 - 1969

By Daisy Lawrenson Swanton

£10.99

Emerging from the Shadow is the story of two generations of women. The diaries of Sarah Lawrenson and her daughter Lucy Kingston give a wonderfully atmospheric picture of life in Wicklow and Dublin - from Dalkey to Rathmines -. in the late nineteenth century.

Sarah Lawrenson courageously supported herself and her family after her husband died leaving her a small inheritance and four young children.

Lucy Kingston campaigned for the rights of women and peace. She became involved in the suffrage movement, the Women's International League for Peace and Freedom and CND. Her story is full of personal social detail and political history

Emerging from the Shadow represents another piece heretofore missing from modern Irish history.

Simply phone us to order your copy or write to:
Attic Press
4 Upper Mount Street, Dublin 2. Ireland.
Tel: (01) 66 16 128   Fax: (01) 66 16 176

Name: _____

Address: _____

_____

_____ Phone No: _____

Total number of books ordered: _____

Books value: £ _____

Add Postage & packing £1.00

Payment enclosed £ _____

Payment by: (please tick) Cheque ☐ Postal Order ☐ (Payable to Attic Press)

Credit Card: (please tick) Visa ☐ Access ☐ Mastercard ☐ Eurocheque ☐

Card No: _ _ _ _ _ _ _ _   Expiry Date: _ _ / _ _